SILVER LAKE COLLEGE LIBRARY

P9-DEI-124

Biegeleisen

5 0 1 7 5

SILVER LAKE COLLEGE LIBRARY
Manitowoc, Wisconsin 54220

screen printing

screen printing

A CONTEMPORARY GUIDE
TO THE TECHNIQUE OF
SCREEN PRINTING
FOR ARTISTS, DESIGNERS,
AND CRAFTSMEN

BY J. I. BIEGELEISEN
ILLUSTRATED BY THE AUTHOR

SILVER LAKE COLLEGE LIBRARY
Manitowoc, Wisconsin 54220

Watson-Guptill Publications, New York

*To my sister Louise whose singular fault
throughout the years has been an immoderate
pride in the accomplishments of her brother.*

Copyright © 1971 by J. I. Biegeleisen
First published 1971 in New York by Watson-Guptill Publications,
a division of Billboard Publications, Inc.,
One Astor Plaza, New York, N.Y. 10036

All rights reserved. No part of this publication
may be reproduced or used in any form or by any means—graphic,
electronic, or mechanical, including photocopying, recording, taping
or information storage and retrieval systems—without
written permission of the publisher.

Manufactured in the U.S.A.

ISBN 0-8230-4665-6
Library of Congress Catalog Card Number: 79-133979

First Printing, 1971
Second Printing, 1973

764.8
B475S

Acknowledgments

Although the material in this book is substantially based on many years of personal experience in screen printing, both as a teacher and practitioner in the field, the book has been appreciably enriched through the help I have received from a large number of sources and individuals.

I would be hard pressed indeed to know whom to thank first—they should all be thanked first—and so I hope to be excused by resorting to an alphabetical listing.

Bill Baker, Union Ink Company; Ben Clements, High School of Art and Design; J. L. Coffey, President, Process Displays Inc.; Harvey Elentuck; Lynn Glicksman, High School of Art and Design; Emil Holden, Active Process Supply Company; Richard Johnson, High School of Art and Design; Lillian Johnston, Prang Studio, The American Crayon Company; Harold Krisel; George Lambert, President, Colonial Printing Ink Company; Guy Maccoy; Frederick Marett, President, The Naz-Dar Company; Steve Poleskie, Cornell University; Herb Prince, Serascreen Corporation; Marian Prince, Ulano Products Company; R. Roger Remington, Rochester Institute of Technology; Joe Slater, Tobler, Ernst & Traber, Inc.; Andrew Stasik, Pratt Center for Contemporary Printmaking; Leslie Tillett; Al Ulano, Serascreen Corporation; and Milton Whelpley.

And to my wife, Esther, who has so ably served as editorial assistant, co-researcher, and full-time collaborator, I want to publicly express my heartfelt gratitude for the role she played in the preparation of this book. I only regret that she did not permit me to include her name on the title page where it rightfully belongs.

3-21-74 EBd $10.60

50175

Contents

Gaps in the design structure are characteristic of the paper and metal stencils employed by early wall and furniture decorators. Some of these stencils are still in use today. Courtesy Delsemme's Artists' Materials Inc., New York.

An example of a Japanese paper stencil shows the use of fine strands of hair for reinforcing and holding together the integral elements of the design image. Courtesy Delsemme's Artists' Materials Inc., New York.

CHAPTER ONE

History of screen printing and its application to the fine arts

Not many years ago, pictorial compositions that were evolved by means of screen stencils were ineligible for submission to major print shows. The primary reason that they weren't acknowledged as authentic prints was that they weren't produced with traditional printing plates. At the same time, and paradoxically enough, they weren't considered acceptable for painting exhibits, because they were summarily classified as prints, not "original" works of art.

Times have changed. So have concepts in art and printmaking. Screen printing today occupies a uniquely ambivalent position both as a creative art medium and as a printmaking technique. As "multiple originals," screen prints—or to put it the other way—works of art evolved through the medium of screen printing are now given prominent space in leading museums and galleries. Among those who make use of the process as a vehicle for their creative efforts are some of our most eminent artists and pacesetters in contemporary art: in the United States, Andy Warhol, Corita Kent, Roy Lichtenstein, Adolph Gottlieb, Robert Indiana, James Rosenquist, Larry Rivers, Jim Dine, and Tom Wesselmann, among others; in Great Britain, artists of the caliber of John Piper, R. B. Kitaj, Bridget Riley, Joe Tilson, and Richard Hamilton; in Germany, Max Ackerman. Screen printing is a fully recognized art form and autographic (that is, original) printing medium in France, Sweden, Germany, Holland, Mexico, Japan, and the world over.

Screen prints as multiple originals (in editions ranging from twenty to 100) are widely purchased by private collectors and by the general public. Prices start at $35 for small prints screened in a few colors and go as high as $500 for large prints in ten to fifteen colors. Feature articles on screen printing as well as reviews of exhibits, appear in prestigious art publications and in the art columns of newspapers. Many art schools and colleges offer studio workshop courses on the subject. It's not an overstatement to say that, as an art medium, screen printing has, indeed, reached a high level of maturity. It had long ago achieved that distinction as a commercial reproduction process.

Let's briefly trace the history of screen printing to see how it all started.

Early Stencilcraft

There's no record of a single individual who can be historically credited with the discovery of stenciling (or screen printing), or who can be compared in stature with Johann Gutenberg, the discoverer of movable type, Alois Senefelder, the discoverer of lithographic printing, or L. J. M. Daguerre, a pioneer in the field of photography.

The principle of screen printing, as we know it today, is a tangential development of stencil techniques employed by artists and artisans throughout the ages. Archaeological findings strongly suggest that many of the repetitive designs that decorated the bleak caves of primitive man were achieved with some form of stenciling A study of the early history of the Fiji Islands brings to light one of the first practical applications of stenciling on fabrics. The islanders prepared their stencils by cutting perforations in broad surfaced banana leaves and then rubbing vegetable dyes through the openings onto bark cloth.

As civilization spread, those interested in the propagation of the faith employed stencils for enhancing religious pictures and psalms. The teachings of Buddha, illuminated with stenciled designs called *image prints,* were thus widely disseminated. Stencilcraft thrived even during the dark period of the Middle Ages. Then, it was used in combination with woodblock printing for such diverse subjects as image prints and playing cards. The closer communication between East and West, which resulted from crusades and conquests, spread the art of stenciling through Europe, from Germany to Spain, Italy, and France. By the sixteenth century, stencilcraft had become an established art and was frequently used as an adjunct to woodblock printing and brush painting. Religious pictures and manuscripts, illuminated by such methods, were widely sold at shrines to the thousands who gathered there at pilgrimages.

In seventeenth century England, when flocked wallpaper was at the height of fashion, stencils were employed to apply the adhesive to the paper. Short fibered flock material, usually of finely cut wool or velour, was sprinkled over the tacky surface to simulate tapestry and other appliqué textures. In France, at the beginning of the eighteenth century, John

Papillon, the father of wallpaper, had established a thriving enterprise for designing and printing wallpaper by the stencil method. In colonial America, stenciling became a favorite medium for applying designs on furniture, directly onto walls, as well as onto wallpaper; the Federal eagle, urns of flowers, baskets of fruit, and vines served as popular motifs.

Stencils were cut from parchment, oil paper, thin metal, or other materials impervious to the coloring matter used. The one identifying characteristic of such stencils was the predominance of gaps in the continuity of the design, brought about by cross-ties or bridges needed to keep the centers of the design from shifting or falling out.

It's the Japanese who are generally credited with developing what might be considered as the forerunner of the *tie-less stencil*. To obviate the need for conspicuous ties, the Japanese stencilmakers long ago perfected a method whereby the fragile and isolated parts of the stencil sheet were held in place by fine strands of silk or human hair. These were painstakingly glued across stencil openings to form a spider-like web, strong enough to hold the stencil, yet so delicate as to be practically invisible in the finished print. The idea of a web or strands as a support may have prompted the later adoption of a permanently stretched fabric to serve as a carrier for the stencil image.

Inception of Screen Printing

It has never been established with any degree of certainty where, or exactly when, printing from the screen stencil first originated. We know that experimental work using fabric as a screen for stenciling was done in Germany and in France as far back as 1870, and then was carried on in England. It's a matter of record that a limited patent relating to screen printing was granted in 1907 to a Samuel Simon of Manchester, England. The Simon patent pertained to the use of a silk screen as a carrier for the stencil, but didn't include a squeegee. Simon employed a brush rather than a rubber squeegee to force the paint through the mesh; this method was somewhat similar to the French *pochoir* celluloid stencil method, which is still practiced in France and elsewhere, for the hand coloring of greeting cards and decorative prints.

Development as a Commercial Craft

Although screen printing had its uncertain beginnings elsewhere, it was in the United States that the process received its greatest impetus as a commercial craft. An active interest in the process developed in this country at about the time of World War I—a period in our history that coincided with the emergence of chain store businesses and the beginning of syndicated point-of-purchase advertising. Chains of ten, twenty, and fifty stores required identical posters, signs, window valances, and advertising banners in quantities too large to be individually painted by hand, yet not large enough to be practical for lithographic or letterpress reproduction. The screen process seemed to be the logical answer.

Enterprising craftsmen and sign and display artists, who anticipated a profitable market, began to experiment with the process. They found it to be an extraordinarily versatile method for duplicating hand lettered work inexpensively, with simple equipment that could easily be constructed in the shop. The screen process enabled them to print on paper, cloth, or cardboard of any weight and size, and in a full range of colors. They could offer not only faster service but also prices considerably lower than the prevailing rates for work rendered by hand or printed by conventional methods.

At first, the *modus operandi* of the process was kept under cover, shared only by a favored few. New developments such as photographic and tusche techniques were jealously guarded shop secrets. These and other "secrets" in time were disseminated within the trade and a fledgling industry was born.

Technological Advances

A very important milestone in screen printing technology was reached in 1929. In that year, an Ohio screen printer named Louis F. D'Autremont introduced Profilm, a shellac stencil film tissue which represented a new and revolutionary concept in stencil preparation. The design image to be reproduced was tracecut on the film with a stencil knife, then adhered to the screen fabric with a warm flatiron. This procedure was not only faster than the predominant methods of tusche and blockout, but (more important) one which produced much sharper printing results than were ever possible before. The advent of the handcut film method of stencil preparation helped to remove one of the serious drawbacks associated with the process as a commercial printing medium: namely, the slightly serrated edges which, in the mind of the advertiser, characterized most of screen printing up to this time.

As innovative as the shellac stencil film tissue was, it was shortly to be replaced. Another type of film, one with a lacquer base, was perfected by Joe Ulano, a noted New York screen printing technician. The Ulano film, and other lacquer handcut films that were subsequently developed, possessed high dimensional stability, were easier to work with, and were simpler to adhere (requiring only a moistening with adhering fluid). These films produced prints characterized by extreme accuracy and literally knife-cut sharpness.

Concurrently with these and other technical advances in stencil preparation, improved ink formulations and automatic printing equipment were developed. All these technological improvements contributed to the ultimate emergence of screen printing as one of the major commercial printing processes.

The Red Tide by Guy Maccoy, courtesy the artist. This print, and the one on the following page, illustrate the effective use of the tusche resist and blockout stencil methods.

King and Queen *by Guy Maccoy, courtesy the artist. Maccoy is one of the pioneers and chief exponents of screen printing as a fine art medium.*

Development as a Fine Art Medium

As a fine art medium, the screen printing process (or, *serigraphy,* as it was later called) is incontrovertibly of American origin. It has its beginnings in the depression era of the 1930's. At that time a group of artists and printmakers met for the purpose of requesting the Works Project Administration (WPA) to establish a unit in screen printing as one of the federally sponsored art projects. The unit, it was pointed out, would provide gainful employment to many in a creative activity; it would be partially, if not wholly, self-sustaining through the production of posters to publicize park department concerts, theatrical performances, and other community-sponsored events. The primary purpose of the unit, however, was to explore the creative aspects of screen printing which could make art prints available to those who couldn't afford to purchase original works of art. The project required a minimum of equipment, comparatively little work space, and could operate on a low budget.

The request was granted, and the unit was established under the leadership of Anthony Velonis, a gifted painter and graphic designer. The newly formed unit turned its full attention to exploring and developing stencil techniques never before attempted by commercial screen printers. The process was redirected into new channels of creativity. Pictorial compositions evolved that were characterized by the ingenious use of tusche and blockout techniques to achieve highly original textural effects as well as linear configurations in a full range of colors. By 1938, two years after the unit was formed, there was already sufficient public interest in screen printing as a fine art medium, and the first one-man show was held at the Contemporary Arts Gallery in New York City. This show featured the work of Guy Maccoy, an outstanding artist and one of the charter members of the WPA group.

Rise of Serigraphy

Soon the works of other exponents of the screen process, such as Edward Landon, Hy Warsager, Elizabeth Olds, Robert Gwathmey, Harry Gottlieb, Leonard Pytlak, and Harry Sternberg, came into public prominence. At first, praise was mixed with skepticism. Among those who expressed unqualified enthusiasm from the very outset was Carl Zigrosser, a noted art historian, and at that time curator of the Philadelphia Museum of Art. It was he who suggested that the term *serigraphy* (Greek: *serikos*—silk; *graphos*—writing) be adopted to identify the screen process when used as a creative art form, in order to distinguish it from its commercial uses in industry. He and Elizabeth McCausland, a visionary art critic and writer of the day, helped through their writings to bring this new art form to the attention of gallery and museum directors in New York and other major cities in the United States.

At about that time, too, (in 1940) the National Serigraph Society was founded, with offices, workshop, and a permanent exhibition gallery located in the heart of New York's art center. The Society, under its director, Doris Meltzer, provided not only a central showcase for serigraphic art, but also included among its many activities a well-coordinated program of lectures, demonstrations, and traveling exhibits. Group and one-man shows were shipped to various parts of the United States as well as to Canada, Cuba, Hawaii, South America, Russia, and Germany. Portfolios of serigraphic prints found their way into such eminent museums as The Metropolitan Museum of Art, The Museum of Modern Art, the Smithsonian Institution, the San Francisco Museum of Art, the Philadelphia Museum of Art, and some of Europe's leading galleries and museums.

Abstract Expressionism: Its Effect on Serigraphy

By 1950, serigraphy was an established art form abroad, but in the United States it had somewhat lost its initial momentum. Practitioners, emboldened by their mastery of techniques, began to employ the process for facile impersonations of other graphic media. The inherent versatility of the process created an irresistible temptation for a number of commercial firms to produce, with a fair degree of credibility, serigraphic prints which simulated the diaphanous transparencies of watercolors, the heavy impasto of oils, or the particular qualities of pastels or woodcuts. Attempts were made (sometimes with drastic results) to reproduce Rembrandts and El Grecos—ambitious undertakings which often required as many as thirty or forty separate printings, enhanced by the addition of brushstroke simulations achieved by means of embossing. These excesses did little to advance serigraphic art either as an artists' reproduction process or as a medium for developing original works of art.

In the United States, the abstract expressionism of the mid-1940's—a movement that dominated the art world for a generation to come was spearheaded by such men as Willem DeKooning, Jackson Pollock, and Franz Kline—began to overshadow in popular appeal the meticulously rendered social realism and genre styles indelibly associated with serigraphy since its early WPA days. The contemporary serigraphers of the day, with notable exceptions, didn't readily fall in line with the new movement, and there was a noticeable decline in serigraphic art between 1950 and 1960. The National Serigraph Society failed to receive sufficient support from artists as well as the general public, and at the end of 1962 discontinued its activities.

The Screen Process and Pop Art

Screen printing as an art form sustained only a temporary setback, and rose to new and unprecedented heights with the ushering in of pop art. It's been said

Self-Portrait by Andy Warhol, 23″ x 23″, edition—300, courtesy Leo Castelli Gallery, New York. A modified photo-stencil method was used to produce this high contrast print. (Photo by Rudolph Burkhardt.)

that Andy Warhol's exhibition of screen printed Campbell Soup boxes in 1962 did more to popularize screen printing than any other single event since Velonis and his group first introduced serigraphy to the art world more than twenty-five years before.

The term *serigraphy* had by this time become an inconsequential distinction between the use of the process as a fine art, as opposed to its baser commercial application. *Screen printing* or *silk screen* was, therefore, eagerly adopted by leading exponents of the movement for one-of-a-kind print creations as well as for multiple productions. Pop art offered no apologia for duplicating processes. Indeed it reflected, through its flaunting satire and superrealism, the tenuous values engendered in a society that thrived on *ready-mades* and duplicates. It was the end product—the final image—that mattered, not how that image was achieved. Artists who employed screen printing made extensive use of commercial techniques which weren't regarded with high favor by earlier fine art practitioners of the process. Handcut film and photographic stencil methods, which were at first almost unequivocally scorned, were adopted as the prime methods for rendering multiple image designs. These stencil methods were used as well for creating the psychedelic double vision compositions associated with optical art. The screen process, in many ways, served not only as an alternate method, but often as the most expedient one by which color could be applied on such difficult to paint surfaces as Plexiglas, burlap, stainless steel, inflatable vinyl, and similar materials.

Poster Art and Art Nouveau

Screen printing received yet another boost in popularity with the revival of art nouveau and the phenomenal popularization of decorative poster art in the mid-1960's. The work of Peter Max must be mentioned in this connection, although there are many others. Like his contemporary, Andy Warhol, Max became one of the most successful exponents of the screen process. His posters were printed in brilliant colors, often in fluorescents. At first—until the quantities ran into the millions—they were produced almost entirely by the screen printing process, and made Peter Max one of the wealthiest young artists in the history of American art.

Screen printing has earned universal acceptance as one of the artist's most versatile idioms for creating, as well as for duplicating works of art. What role is waiting for it in the distant future? Only time will tell.

Brushstroke on Benday Dots *by Roy Lichtenstein, 23″ x 29″, courtesy Leo Castelli Gallery, New York. The artist selected the photostencil method to achieve this bold comic strip pop art effect.*

Plexiglas Montage *by Larry Rivers, courtesy Multiples Inc., New York. The versatility of screen printing is in evidence in this unusual multicolor design screened on layers of Plexiglas.*

CHAPTER TWO

Setting up shop

Once you've assembled your basic screen printing equipment, you'll have at your disposal what's generally considered the most versatile printing process in the entire field of graphic arts. You'll be able to print in black and white and full color, on paper, cardboard, glass, metal, plastic sheets, cloth—even on ½" heavy plywood. On anything, in fact, regardless of the nature or thickness of material, as long as the printing surface is fairly flat. You'll learn later on how round or irregularly shaped objects can also be screened with special jigs and simple auxiliary equipment.

The process is good for any number of copies: a hundred, a thousand, or ten times that many. You may, of course, limit your edition to just a handful of prints if that's all you require.

Color Possibilities

All the colors in the rainbow are yours to choose from. Screen inks come in an array of standard colors and shades. There are screen inks which are formulated to be opaque, making it possible to print a light color over a dark color in one operation. For instance, gleaming white ink can be printed over a jet black ground, or a bright yellow over a deep brown without loss of chroma. If you prefer to work with transparent tints, that's no particular problem. Opaque inks can be easily made transparent with an additive that doesn't change the intensity of the color; the additive just makes it transparent. Thus, transparent blue printed on a white background, still retains its original hue; printed over yellow, the resulting color is green. Similarly, red over black will come out brown; yellow over red will produce orange, and so on.

You'll have considerable latitude, not merely in the degree of opacity (or transparency) of the ink, but in the finish as well: from a dull matte to a highly reflective gloss, depending upon the type of printing medium you choose. Oil based inks, those designed primarily for poster reproduction, are the most popular, but these inks by no means constitute the only printing medium. For instance, emulsion pigments and dyes are generally reserved for textiles; lacquers and synthetic inks for plastics; and adhesive compounds for flock and tinsel effects. For some purposes acrylics may be best; for others, tempera paints. In short, you can print with practically any viscous substance that can go through the mesh of a screen. You may even decide to print with an etching compound that produces a permanent frosting on glass.

Design Sizes

As to maximum size of the design that can be reproduced, there's virtually no "maximum." Unlike other printing processes where the printing area is necessarily limited by the size of the press, in screen printing there's no such fixed restriction. You simply construct the screen unit to fit the dimensions of the design to be reproduced. It's not the other way around.

Assembling the Screen Unit

You can make the screen unit yourself, or buy it ready-made, completely assembled. Either way, the screen unit represents a permanent facility and is good for any number of colors and for many different design projects. The unit is portable, and takes up little storage space. The cost for assembling it is low, compared to printing methods which require presses or other heavy equipment.

In the main, the printing unit consists of a screen frame hinged at one end to a flat baseboard, enabling the screen frame to be moved up and down. The screen *element* is the silk (or other fabric) stretched and tacked across the frame. To complete the basic printing unit—namely screen and baseboard—you'll need a squeegee, the implement used to push the ink through the openings of the stencil. More about this later.

The Screen Frame

The frame serves two functions: as a rectangular hoop it keeps the screen fabric stretched nice and tight; it also serves as a trough for the printing ink.

Most screen frames are constructed of wood. Screen printers of specialty items such as glass and

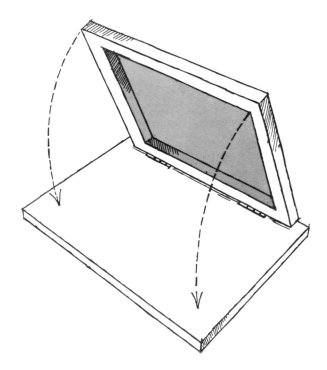

The printing unit consists of a screen frame hinged at one end to a flat baseboard, enabling the screen frame to be raised and lowered.

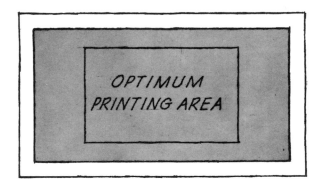

OPTIMUM PRINTING AREA

The inside measurements of the screen frame must be considerably larger than the maximum dimensions of the printing area.

ceramicware, and printed circuits, occasionally employ cast aluminum frames. In the display and poster field, however, and among artists who do their own screen printing, wood frames are standard.

You can buy frames ready-made, or get your local carpentry shop to make them up to your specifications. It's simple enough to build a frame, and if you're at all handy with hammer and saw, you'll probably prefer making it yourself.

Let's assume that you decide to build your own, and proceed from there.

Type of wood: Strips for the frame can be purchased at any lumberyard. The wood must be soft enough to take staples or tacks, yet firm enongh to withstand the considerable stress put on it by the stretched fabric.

For small frames, ¾" x 1¼" firring strips are acceptable and comparatively inexpensive. White pine, which is a little higher priced, is superior because it's smoother surfaced and somewhat stronger. Whichever type or size of wood you get, it's important that it be free from knots and warping. For jumbo-sized frames, 40" x 60", and larger, 1" x 2" (or heavier) kiln dried, hardwood strips are recommended. Understandably, the larger the frame, the heavier and stronger the wood strips ought to be to withstand the pull of the screen fabric.

Frame dimensions: The size of the frame is optional, but bear in mind that the inside measurements must be considerably larger than the maximum dimensions of the printing area.

Just *how much* larger? The sketch shown here will give you an idea of the recommended relationship between frame size and optimum printing area.

You'll note that a lot of marginal space is allowed on the two sides—much more than on top and bottom. That's because in printing, the squeegee is pushed from side to side, rather than from top to bottom. Adequate space, therefore, must be provided on both sides of the screen to serve as a reservoir for the ink as it's pushed from one side to the other with each crossing of the squeegee.

Corner joints: The trick in putting the screen frame together is to get rigid joinings of the four strips. The end result should be a frame that won't twist, and lies absolutely flat. Complicated corner joints aren't necessary.

There are many ways to join the corners of a frame. You can use a double-lap joint, a simple butt joint, a half-lap joint, or a mitered joint, to mention just a few.

In each type of joint, corners can be further strengthened by dabbing glue on the joinings, and by using angle irons.

The frame isn't finished until all sides are sanded down well and given a protective coat of lacquer or shellac. This treatment seals the wood and prevents it from warping. It also makes the frame easier to keep clean.

The Baseboard

This is the equivalent of a platen or bed—terms used in letterpress printing and other graphic arts. The baseboard (or to adopt the jargon of the trade, the "bed") fixes the position of the screen and serves as a flat surface for the placement and registering of the paper or other stock to be printed.

There are no strict rules for preparing the bed. It can be ½" or ¾" pine, plywood, or similar material. A flat tabletop or artist's drawing board will do as well. The type of wood or its exact thickness is of no great consequence. What *is* important is that the surface be absolutely flat and smooth. An uneven, rough surface makes for trouble in printing, especially on thin stock.

It's a good idea to give the bed a good going over with sandpaper, and then give it a coat of lacquer or shellac. This procedure is used for the same reasons (to prevent warping and facilitate cleaning) that were suggested for finishing the screen frame. Some printers make it a practice to protect the bed, and further assure its smoothness, by covering it with a sheet of heavy cardboard. As to size, the bed should be several inches larger all around than the outer dimensions of the screen frame.

The Hinges

"Pushpin" hinges—similar to ordinary door hinges—are used to attach the frame to the bed. They come in different sizes and are readily obtainable at any local hardware or five-and-dime store. Two pairs are needed: one goes on the long end of the frame; the other goes on the bed. A pair of hinges consists of two interlocking metal plates (male and female) held together by a rod-like pin.

In hinging the frame, first remove the pin, separating the two plates. Fasten the female plate at one end of the frame, and the male plate at the other end, about two or three inches away from each edge. That done, visually center the frame on the bed. Using another pair of hinges, fasten the counterpart of each plate to the bed so that the hinge-mates on the frame interlock with those on the bed.

If your inventory eventually includes a number of frames of approximately the same size, they can all be made to fit the hinges on the master bed.

A point to remember: by having one male and one female plate permanently fastened to the master bed, only one pair of hinges is required per frame. If two male plates were fastened to the bed, each frame would require two female plates and their male counterparts would have to be discarded.

You may be interested in trying a clamp-type hinge instead of a push pin hinge. Though this clamp-type hinge hasn't gained wide acceptance, it has much to recommend it. Mainly it eliminates the need of attaching hinges to the screen frame. The clamp hinge is adjustable; it holds a screen up to 2" thick. Screens are engaged or disengaged by a simple wing nut adjustment.

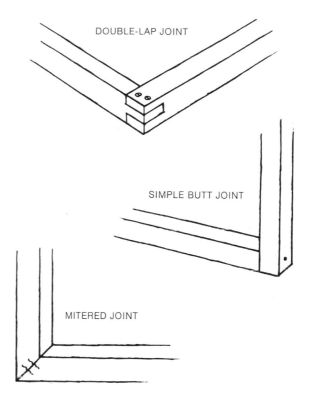

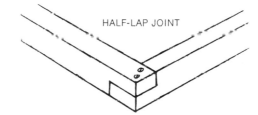

Here are just four of the many ways to join the corners of a screen frame.

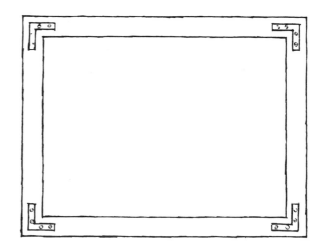

Angle irons fastened to screen frame corners help to reinforce the frame and add to its rigidity.

SILVER LAKE COLLEGE LIBRARY

Manitowoc, Wisconsin 54220

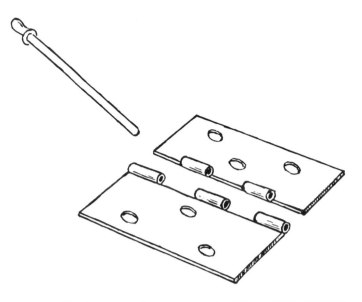

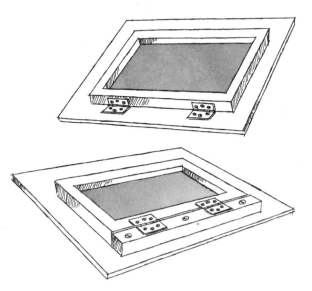

The two parts of a pushpin-type screen hinge interlock and are held together with a connecting rod.

Top Illustration: The standard procedure is to hinge the screen frame directly to the printing bed as shown here. Bottom Illustration: An optional procedure is to hinge the screen frame to a strip of wood or "back bar" fastened to the printing bed.

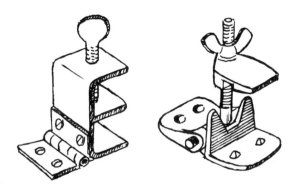

Adjustable screen frame clamps, such as these, allow screens to be engaged or disengaged by simply turning a wing nut.

A closeup view of an adjustable clamp-type hinge shows the manner in which the screen frame is attached to the printing bed.

Silk and Other Screen Fabrics

The fabric employed in screen printing is porous. So are all fabrics woven with a mesh structure. Ink, or other fluid compounds, spread or rubbed over such fabrics will seep through. The rate of penetration will depend on the viscosity of the ink, the size of the mesh opening, what you use to squeegee it through, and how hard you press. What makes the fabric used in screen printing so special? It keeps taut once it's stretched on the frame; the mesh is uniform; and although the fibers are very thin, they possess remarkable tensile strength. Incredible as it may seem, most screen fabrics are able to withstand the action of alkalis, acids, solvents, lacquers, dyes, and various other printing mediums. With normal care, a screen will last for thousands of impressions, unimpaired by the constant passing of the squeegee, even with pressure. You're likely to wear out the tough rubber blade of the squeegee sooner than you'll wear out the screen fabric.

Silk fabrics are classified by the size of the mesh —the working range being from #8XX to #18XX, with #12XX considered the medium and most popular mesh size. Fabrics come in mesh sizes even higher than #18XX, but anything above #12XX is generally reserved for unusually fine detail and photographic halftone reproduction. The XX designation signifies "double extra"—the fiber weight recommended for most screen printing purposes.

There are charts which scientifically tabulate the exact number of meshes per linear inch, the size openings of the mesh, percentage of open area, etc. Thus, #12XX silk (previously referred to) has a mesh count of 125, an aperture size of .0045, and an open area of 32%. A silk classified as #16XX has a mesh count of 157, an aperture size of .0035, an open area of 31%, and so on. These tabulations, however, normally have little practical relevance to your needs at this time. What's important for you to know is that the higher the number, the finer and smaller the mesh.

When you've gained more knowledge of the screen process through practical experience, you'll most likely want to experiment with a wider range of screen fabrics, not only in terms of mesh size, but in the nature of the fabric as well.

For many years, natural silk was the most widely used of screen fabrics and is still the choice of many practitioners in the field. Indeed, the term silk screen printing—which for a long time identified the process, and still does to a great extent—is derived from an earlier day when silk was almost the universal screen fabric used. With the passing of time, however, more and more use has been made of nylon, dacron, and other synthetic fibers, as well as finely woven metal fabrics made of stainless steel and copper. Each of these has its own working characteristics and requires somewhat special handling in stretching, stencil preparation, care, and maintenance.

Silk (as well as some of the other fabrics mentioned) is sold in standard widths, ranging from 40" to as much as 80". Lengths are cut to any size specified, although dealers prefer to sell by the yard.

The cost of silk varies considerably; the range is from about $4 to as high as $10 per yard. The price depends upon width of material, size of mesh opening, and quality of fabric. Generally speaking, the best screen silks are imported from Switzerland, Holland, and Japan, and cost proportionately more than the domestic kind.

At first glance, the price of silk admittedly appears rather high. However, at an average cost of say $7 per yard, one yard of 50" silk will give you more than ample material for covering two 20" x 30" screens. With proper care, these will last for years without replacement.

Organdy (which can be bought at a fraction of the price of silk) may be used as a screen fabric with the understanding that it has inherent limitations. For one thing, it lacks the tensile strength and durability of silk and cannot be stretched as tightly without the danger of tearing. Then too, it can't be successfully used with any ink or compound which has a water base. Water tends to slacken the tautness of the fabric, impairing the quality of the print and the accuracy of register.

Stretching the Screen Fabric

There are a number of different ways to stretch the fabric on the frame. Whichever way you adopt, you must end up with a screen that's as taut as a drum. There are screen printers in the field who are fully convinced that the only way to stretch the screen correctly is their way; you may, in time, become one of them yourself. Meanwhile, here's *one* way, let's say, one of many.

Step 1: Cut the fabric several inches larger than the outer dimensions of the frame. (There's no right or wrong side to the fabric; either side may be used.)

Lay the fabric over the frame, placing the selvage edge flush with side A, as shown. Bear in mind, in preparing a screen, that the fabric is fastened to the *face* of the frame, not around the edges, as is the custom in stretching artists' canvas.

Step 2: Using #4 carpet tacks (or heavy staples), fasten the fabric to side A, spacing the tacks about an inch or so apart. Pull the fabric taut, as you drive in each tack. Sometimes, it's best to start in the center of the frame, alternately placing a tack on each side of center, until the entire side is completed.

Step 3: Tack side B. With a firm grip on the fabric, pull from the center out diagonally.

Step 4: Tack side C (or D). This calls for somewhat less pull, but be sure that you don't leave any slack or wrinkles.

Step 5: Tack the opposite (and last) side, gripping the fabric as tightly as you can with a diagonal pull from the center out.

Screen Fabric Comparison Chart

SCREEN	MESH COUNT			MESH OPENING			PERCENT OPEN AREA		
	*SILK	NYLON	WIRE	*SILK	NYLON	WIRE	*SILK	NYLON	WIRE
6XX	74	70	70	.0094"	.0094"	.0106"	47	44.5	55
8XX	86	90	88	.0077"	.0071"	.0079"	45	41.5	48
10XX	109	108	105	.0057"	.0059"	.0065"	40	43.0	47
12XX	125	120	120	.0045"	.0055"	.0057"	32	44.5	47
14XX	139	138	135	.0038"	.0049"	.0051"	30	46.5	47
16XX	157	157	145	.0035"	.0041"	.0047"	31	40.5	46
18XX	166	166	165	.0031"	.0037"	.0042"	31	37.5	47
20XX	173	185	180	.0030"	.0035"	.0041"	28	43.0	47
25XX	200	196	200	.0025"	.0033"	.0034"	23	44.0	46
		230	230		.0028"	.0029"		42.0	46
		240	250		.0026"	.0024"		39.0	36
		260	270		.0023"	.0021"		36.0	32
		283			.0022"			37.0	
		306			.0019"			33.5	
		330	325		.0017"	.0017"		30.0	30
		380	400		.0012"	.0015"		21.5	36
			508			.0010"			25

*Note: Dacron (multifilament) same specifications as silk.

 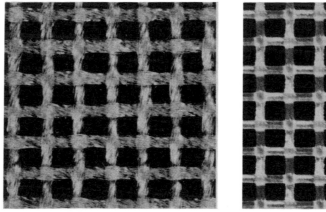 

The most popular screen fabrics (shown here highly magnified) are: Left: Tafetta or Plain Weave Silk; Middle: Dacron Multifilament; and Right: Nylon Monofilament. Photo courtesy Tobler, Ernst and Traber, Inc., Elmsford, New York.

Step 6: Neatly trim the excess fabric that overhangs the edges of the frame. Then, brush a coat of lacquer (or shellac) over the tacked areas, going half an inch or thereabouts into the open mesh. Be careful not to spatter or drip the lacquer.

One of the hazards that confronts the beginner in stretching fabric on the screen is that, in his attempt to exert maximum pull on the fabric, it may develop rips at the stretch points. However, with experience he'll be able to instinctively gauge the amount of tension that the fabric will withstand without ripping or tearing.

If you've stretched canvas on a frame, and employed a pliers stretcher with success, you may want to use the same type of pliers to help you stretch the screen fabric.

Taping the Screen

Paste strips of water moistened 2″ gum paper tape (the kind used for packages) over each of the tacked surfaces, overlapping them partly into the screen. Rub the strips down well, and make every effort to press out trapped air bubbles. Cover the strips with a coat of lacquer or shellac.

The binding procedure helps to reinforce the anchorage of the fabric to the frame and, at the same time, provides a neat covering for the tacked surfaces.

Next, turn the frame over (fabric side down), and bind the inside of the frame where fabric and wood meet. This time, crease each strip of gum paper in half, lengthwise. Paste the gum paper down so that one half lies flat on the fabric and the other half fits snugly against the inside edge of the frame. Then, reinforce the four corners with small strips of gum paper folded L-shape to fit snugly, and press down well. Finish with a coat of lacquer or shellac, just as you did on the other side.

Binding seals the screen all along the edges where fabric and frame meet and is a precautionary measure against the leakage of ink during printing.

Screen Lifting Devices

There are any number of devices used to keep the screen in a raised position during the intervals before and after the print is made.

No doubt the simplest one consists of ½″ x ¼″ strip of wood, 8″ to 10″ long, attached to one side of the frame so that it hangs loosely on a nail or screw. The wood support (or *drop stick* as it's called) should drop down freely by its own weight when the screen is raised; it should keep the screen propped up at about a 25° angle.

For limited editions, the drop stick is adequate; for extended production runs there are more sophisticated devices, some of which are: the adjustable counterweight lift, the door hinge lift, the pulley lift, and the automatic coil spring, side stick lift.

Shown here in six sequential steps is a suggested procedure for stretching the screen fabric.

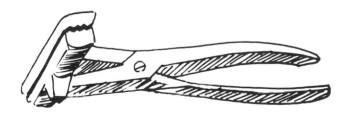

A pair of pull pliers serves as a handy device for stretching the screen fabric.

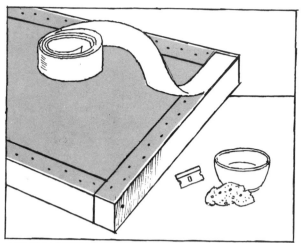

Lengths of gum paper are cut to fit the frame.

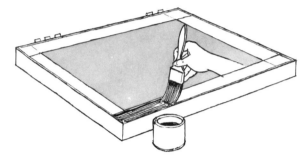

A coat of lacquer or shellac applied over the gum paper binding provides added security against ink seepage and facilitates cleaning the screen frame after printing.

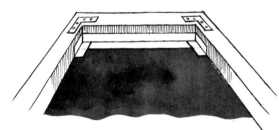

An inside view of the screen shows the placement of gum paper binding between screen frame and fabric.

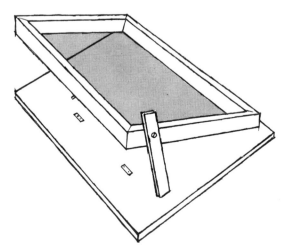

A simple side stick support drops down by its own weight when the screen is raised.

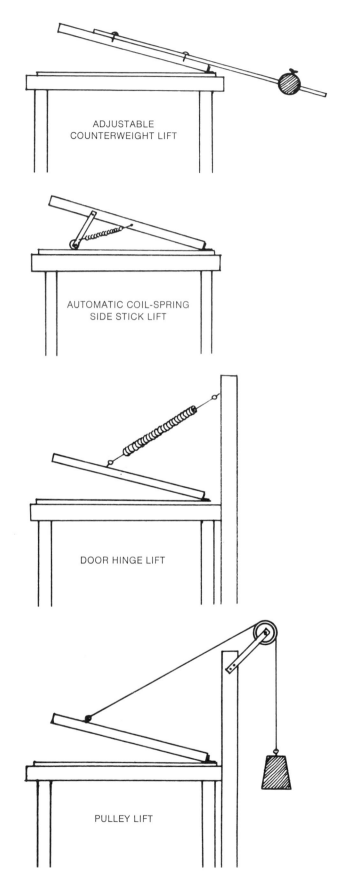

ADJUSTABLE
COUNTERWEIGHT LIFT

AUTOMATIC COIL-SPRING
SIDE STICK LIFT

DOOR HINGE LIFT

PULLEY LIFT

These schematic drawings are suggestive of the many mechanical lifts that can be devised for raising the screen.

The Squeegee

The squeegee is composed of a strip of durable rubber belting partly encased in a wood or metal holder, with the rubber extending about 1¼". The working part of the squeegee is the rubber belting or blade. The casing keeps the rubber blade firm, and also provides a gripping space for the hand.

You can construct the casing yourself and buy the rubber separately, or you may, of course, purchase a ready-made squeegee. Squeegees are sold by the linear inch in any length you require. The price varies with the quality of the rubber and the kind of casing preferred.

To determine the size of the squeegee you need, measure the inside width of the screen frame, and subtract an inch or so. The squeegee must be somewhat smaller than the inside width of the screen frame to allow for adequate up and down play of the squeegee as it's pushed across the length of the screen. If the squeegee is too large, you won't be able to scrape it side to side (as you should). If it's too small, it won't cover the area in one scrape.

For a screen area 15" x 24" (inside dimensions), the squeegee might well be about 13" or 14". Understandably, a squeegee this size would be good for a screen of any length, provided the inside width is not appreciably less than 15".

The squeegee we've been talking about is the type that's gripped with both hands—known in the trade as a "two-hand squeegee." This is the kind you'll probably find easiest to use. The one-hand squeegee (which is pushed across the screen with one hand) comes equipped with a grip handle fastened to the center of the casing.

The rubber belting used in squeegees is generally 2" wide and ⅜" thick, and comes in different degrees of pliability—soft, medium, and hard. To start, all you need is a squeegee with medium rubber, which is serviceable for most printing projects.

It takes thousands of impressions for the rubber blade to show signs of wear. When the blade begins to dull, a dozen or so strokes over a sandpaper or garnet board surface will restore the edge. If properly cleaned after use, the squeegee will last for years.

Drying Facilities

Most inks and other compounds used in screen printing don't dry quickly enough to permit putting prints on top of each other, as soon as they come off the printing bed. Facilities, therefore, must be provided for keeping the wet prints separated until they've had a chance to dry.

For an edition consisting of just a handful of prints, you can easily manage by laying the wet prints about the room. If you plan larger editions, you may want to improvise more elaborate drying facilities, or purchase other professional drying equipment.

With this basic equipment assembled, you're ready to proceed with stencil preparation.

TWO-HAND SQUEEGEE

ONE-HAND SQUEEGEE

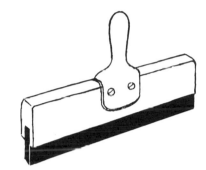

TYPES OF RUBBER EDGES FOR SQUEEGEES

Both the one-hand and two-hand squeegees can be fitted with various rubber edges (from left to right). Square Edge: for printing on most flat stock; Square Edge with Rounded Corners: used whenever a heavier-than-usual deposit of ink is required; Double-Sided Bevel Edge: for printing on bottles, containers, and round or uneven surfaces; Rounded Edge: used mostly for textile printing where a deep penetration of color is needed; Double-Sided Bevel Edge, Flat Point: for ceramicware.

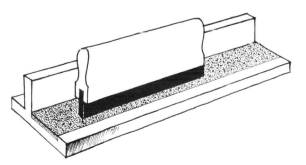

A sandpaper block is useful for sharpening the squeegee rubber.

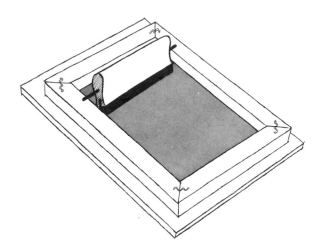

Protruding dowels or rods on either end of the squeegee prevent it from toppling into the ink reserve in the screen, yet they don't interfere with the normal operation of the squeegee.

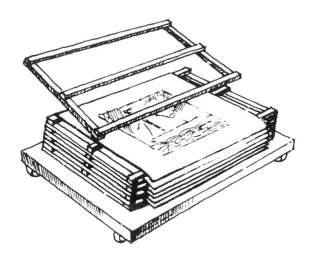

Wood-slat frame racks, made uniform in size to stack up neatly on a rolling platform or dolly, are good for flexible as well as for rigid printing surfaces.

The cross stick on the one-hand squeegee accomplishes the same objective as the extension rods on the two-hand squeegee—namely, to keep the squeegee from falling into the ink reserve.

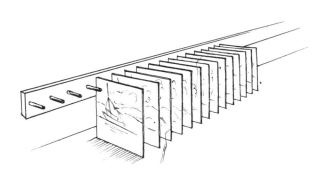

Prints made on heavy cardboard or rigid material may be stacked upright against nails or dowels spaced on a baseboard or a strip of wood fastened to the wall.

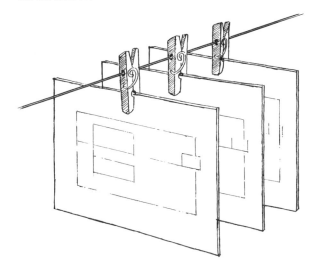

This clothesline off-floor drying arrangement uses wire cable strung through holes in clothespins.

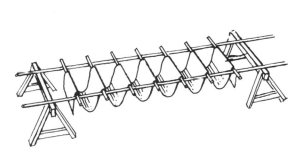

A festoon-type parallel bar arrangement is good for drying long paper signs, piece goods, and other flexible stock.

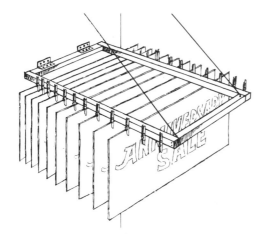

A simple rack device composed of an overhang frame may be raised out of the way when not in use. Clothespins nailed to the sides of the frame hold prints during the drying interval.

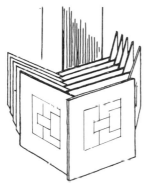

"Domino" type floor stacking against a post or other upright support is possible if the printing stock is rigid and of a heavy gauge.

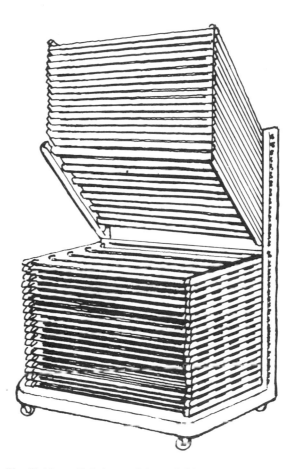

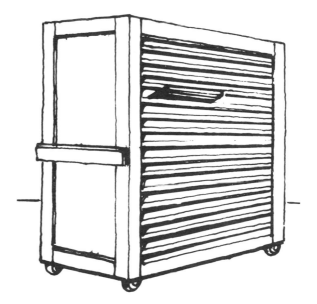

The "fold-over" drying rack is available in wood or metal, and comes in a number of sizes. The rack's self-balancing, tension spring construction permits trays to be raised or lowered for easy placement and removal of prints.

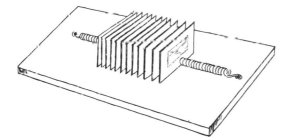

A spring affixed to a baseboard serves as an upright stacking device for drying prints on rigid material.

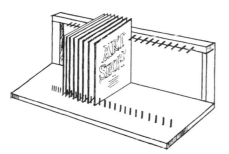

Two rows of nails or dowels—one on a flat board and the other on an upright support—provide the limited edition screen printer with a portable tabletop drying unit.

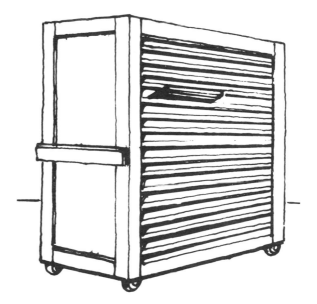

This multiple drying rack unit is constructed with evenly spaced trays set in a fixed position.

This screen printing setup includes a pulley system for raising the screen, a professional drying rack, and provisions for overhead storage of screen frames.

CHAPTER THREE

Introduction to stencil making techniques

The printing unit that you've assembled doesn't become operational until the screen is partially blocked out to form a stencil. A printed image of the design is created when ink, or other media squeegeed across the screen, drops through the areas left open. The mesh supporting the component elements of the stencil eliminates the need for the conspicuous ties or bridges traditionally associated with a stenciled image. The strands of silk (or other meshed fabric) which comprise the screen serve as a webwork of ties so exceedingly fine that they're virtually invisible in the finished print.

Blocking Out the Screen

The different ways in which the open screen can be blocked out to create a printing image constitute the basic stencil making techniques. Blocking out, as you'll see later, may be done with paper, film tissue, a colloid such as glue, or may be achieved photographically. Each method has its unique advantages and limitations. Each has its own procedure and yields a graphic quality all its own.

Stencil Methods and Personal Preference

The various stencil making methods can be used interchangeably, or, they can be combined. As you become more familiar with the screen process, you'll most likely show a preference for those stencil techniques which are most sensitive to your personal style.

Glue, in conjunction with a resist compound, is favored by such notable serigraphic artists as Corita Kent and Guy Maccoy.

The highly original collage screen prints of R. B. Kitaj achieve added dramatic effects through the adroit use of photographic techniques.

Harold Krisel has consistently shown a preference for the film method to reproduce his colorful geometric compositions. His work is characterized by a sharp definition of color boundaries—a precise, hard-edge style admirably suited for film tissue as a blockout medium.

Norio Azuma, who often screens directly on canvas in as many as twenty colors, makes use of cut paper as a blockout medium. He capitalizes on the slightly raised edges of the paper to produce an impasto collage effect.

Commercially, most stencils today are made photographically or with handcut stencil films.

Although in practice the different methods are often combined to contribute to the technical and aesthetic evolvement of a design image, five principal stencil making methods will be discussed here separately, with a chapter devoted to each.

Love is Here to Stay by Corita Kent, courtesy the artist. A blockout fluid such as glue or lacquer applied directly to the open screen can prove to be an effective medium for creating a strong negative image in lettering or design.

(Above) The Cultural Value of Fear, Distrust, and Hypochondria by R. B. Kitaj, courtesy Marlborough Graphics, Inc., New York. Photographic stencils play an important role in the various techniques employed to reproduce the highly imaginative collages of this outstanding artist.

(Right) The Town by Norio Azuma, stretched canvas, courtesy the artist. Azuma uses fourteen oil colors, screened directly onto the canvas, and the paper stencil method to achieve a highly effective impasto impression.

(Above) A & D Anniversary Poster by A. C. Hollingsworth, courtesy the artist. This three color poster was reproduced with photostencils prepared by the artist, and screen printed by the Graphic Arts Workshop students of the High School of Art and Design.

(Right) Sailing Craft in Harbor by Martin J. Weber, courtesy Martin J. Weber Studio, New York. This posterized illustration was screened in four colors from photostencils using specially prepared color separation transparencies.

Winona *by Steve Poleskie, courtesy the Pratt Center for Contemporary Printmaking, New York. Produced with handcut film stencils, this print shows a highly disciplined simplicity in color and design—a distinguishable feature of the work of this popular artist and printmaker.*

CHAPTER FOUR

The blockout stencil method

Broadly speaking, any method employed in screen printing reproduction whereby a stencil is created, may be classified as a blockout method. This is true irrespective of the nature of the medium employed to block out the open screen—whether it's glue, paper, film tissue, photographic emulsion, or another substance. In the language of the craft, however, the term *blockout method* has a more restricted meaning; it applies specifically to that procedure whereby a hard drying fluid such as glue, lacquer, or shellac is brushed directly on the screen, blocking out some parts and leaving others open to form a stencil image. The open parts represent the positive or *printing* areas; the blocked out parts represent the negative or *non-printing* areas.

The blockout method of stencil preparation has been largely replaced by handout film and modern photographic techniques for printing of posters, point-of purchase displays, and for various other commercial uses where a precise, sharp line and an exact reproduction fidelity are essential. The blockout method has remained, however, one of the favorite methods utilized by serigraphic artists, because of the inviting opportunities it offers for individual treatments and varied textural improvisations. Prints made with blockout stencils are characterized by a soft-edge quality induced to some extent by the fibrous mesh of the screen fabric, but particularly, by the responsiveness of the blockout medium to stipple, spatter, drybrush, and other art techniques.

Making a Glue Blockout Stencil

For limited edition printing, glue, as a blockout medium, has much to recommend it. It's easy to work with and responds readily to varied art treatments in creating the stencil image on the screen. It's comparatively inexpensive, noncombustible and requires no chemical solvent to remove the stencil image and reclaim the screen.

The procedure outlined below for preparing a blockout stencil will make particular reference to glue as the blockout medium, with the understanding that lacquer, shellac, or other compounds can be used as well.

Note that in this and the other chapters dealing with stencil making techniques, the hypothetical design to be reproduced will, for the sake of instructional clarity, be confined to a single color. The technical aspects of multicolor work—how to reproduce a design in two or more colors and get them to register properly—are treated in full in Chapter 9.

Step 1. Position the art on the bed: Place the art in a horizontal position on the printing bed, centering it visually under the screen. *Note* that in this and other handmade stencil methods, the art should be the same size as the intended reproduction and should correspond to the size of the edition stock.

Step 2. Set the register guides: Staple, tape, or otherwise affix three small cardboard or metal tabs to the bed to serve as register guides. These are fitted snugly against the art: one goes along the lower left side (as you face the screen); the other two go along the bottom at a sizable distance from each other.

Step 3. Trace the art: With the art securely set in the guides and screen lowered, make a comprehensive pencil or ink tracing of all elements of the design as you see them through the screen.

Step 4. Code the tracing: Draw an x mark (or other convenient symbol) within the various elements of the traced design to signify which parts of the screen are to be blocked out, and which are to be left open.

Step 5. Set up for gluing: Raise the screen slightly at the front end. Prop it up, about ½" above the bed, so that the screen fabric doesn't touch the surface below. At this point, the art may be removed from the bed, or left in position, if it has been covered with a sheet of transparent acetate. The acetate protects the art from possible glue seepage, and, at the same time, allows it to be in constant view during the course of stencil preparation. Use a good grade fish-type, water-soluble glue, such as LePage's Full Strength Liquid Glue. Thin it to a convenient brushing consistency (about one part full-strength glue to one part water). You may add a drop of tempera paint or water color to the glue mixture to make it more visually contrasting with the screen surface.

Image of the Yellowstone *by R. Roger Remington, courtesy the artist. Improvisation played an important role in producing this exuberant color collage, where screen printing was employed not merely as a reproduction process, but as a creative art medium as well.*

Step 6. Glue in the stencil image: Apply the glue mixture to all traced areas on the screen that correspond to the nonprinting (negative) elements of the stencil image. Use a small brush for the outlines, and a larger one for filling in. Allow to air-dry naturally. You may speed up the drying with the aid of a fan. When dry, the glue forms a hard, impenetrable film.

Step 7. Check the stencil: Raise the screen, holding it vertically to a source of light, and check carefully for leaks or pinholes. Where necessary, touch up with a dab of glue. When that's done, the stencil is ready for printing.

A Word About Printing

Printing from a glue blockout stencil is no different than printing from other screen stencils. The procedure for making the stencil varies, not the printing.

The procedure for printing is described fully in Chapter 12, but here, very briefly, is how it's done.

Place the card (or other stock) to be printed in the register guides on the bed and lower the screen. Pour the ink into one side of the screen and push the squeegee across, forcing the ink through the stencil openings onto the stock below. Each crossing of the squeegee produces a print.

When the edition is finished, scoop up the ink remaining in the screen and place it back in the container. Then clean the screen and squeegee with the proper solvent.

Durability of a Glue Blockout Stencil

A stencil made with glue as a blockout medium can be expected to yield 150 to 200 good impressions. After that amount clusters of tiny pinholes are likely to develop as the glue begins to break down under repeated crossings of the squeegee. The pinholes can, of course, be masked out on the screen as they crop up, but then a blockout stencil made with glue *is not* intended for extended editions. There are more durable blockout media that can be used, and other stencil making techniques that are better suited for extended editions.

When glue is employed as the blockout medium, the stencil can be printed with all standard screen inks, except tempera paints and certain textile dyes formulated on a water based principle. After the printing is completed, the stencil may be stored away for a re-run. If no further editions are planned, the screen may easily be reclaimed by washing it with water. When the glue dissolves, the stencil image on the screen disintegrates, clearing the mesh. The reclaimed screen can be used for subsequent color stencils of the same basic design or for any number of completely new design projects.

For more durable blockout stencils that are suitable for long edition printing, lacquer, shellac, and film forming compounds other than glue are recommended. Such stencils, however, can't be reclaimed

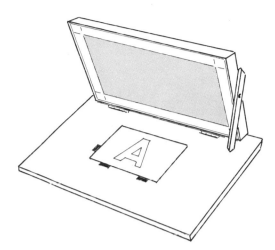

Positioning the artwork in the register guides.

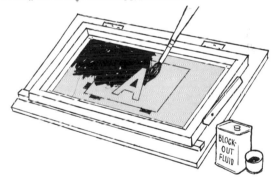

Tracing the design on the screen fabric.

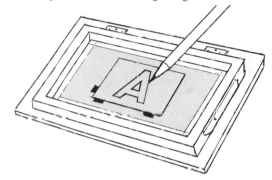

Applying blockout fluid to the nonprinting areas.

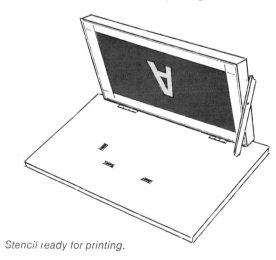

Stencil ready for printing.

Gold Face Type by Emma Amos, courtesy Associated American Artists, New York. A combination of tusche and blockout stencil techniques was arttully employed in producing this limited edition screen print.

quite as easily as those made with glue, unless the screen is coated with a sizing prior to applying the blockout fluid.

Sizing the Screen for Other Blockout Media

Sizing the screen also has its advantages. No tracing is necessary. The sizing (which temporarily fills the mesh) makes it possible to work directly over the art, because it prevents the blockout fluid from seeping through the screen. A sized screen also yields somewhat sharper prints.

To size the screen, prop it up so that it doesn't touch the surface below. Then with a stiff, sharp-edged piece of cardboard as a scraper, coat the entire top surface of the screen with a diluted glue solution, made up of one part glue plus three parts water. You'll note that the glue solution used as a *sizing* is of a considerably thinner consistency than the glue used as a *blockout medium.*

When the sizing is dry, paint in on the screen fabric the nonprinting areas of the stencil with lacquer, shellac, or similar water resistant blockout fluid. The art below is clearly visible, since the sizing hardly—if at all—affects the natural see-through visibility of the screen fabric. Now remove the art and allow the stencil to dry. When the blockout medium is dry, the glue sizing in the printing areas of the stencil is ready to be dissolved. To do this, pass a water saturated sponge over the top surface of the screen. Don't let any water drip through to the underside directly below the blockout areas. Then, with a dry, absorbent cloth, remove any vestige of water or residual glue that may be lodged within the printing areas of the design image. The removal of the sizing opens the stencil, making it ready for printing.

In reclaiming a glue-sized screen, all that's necessary to remove the stencil image is to, first, rinse the underside with cold water. Then, follow up with a water wash on top. When the glue foundation upon which the blockout medium rests is dissolved, the blockout medium has nothing to hold onto, and consequently flakes off, clearing the mesh.

Blockout Fluids

Although glue, lacquer, and shellac are the three principal blockout mediums, other fluids such as varnish, caustic resist enamel, and polyurethane can be used.

Glue: Employed as a blockout medium, glue must be of the fish-type variety, the kind that responds to water as a thinning agent and solvent. A good grade of glue dries quickly, forming a strong, flexible film, and shows no tendency towards brittleness. As it comes in the container, glue is generally too thick to be applied to the screen without thinning. When used as a *blockout medium,* glue should be thinned to the brushing consistency of tempera paint. When used as a *sizing,* glue should be far more free flowing, somewhat of the consistency of light cream.

A stencil made with glue can be printed with oil based inks, lacquers, enamels, and certain non-water-soluble textile inks. It can't be used with any printing ink which contains water.

To reclaim a glue blockout stencil all that's required is a washing with water, either cold or warm. Water will also clean brushes, sponges, and other art tools used in preparing the stencil.

Lacquer: Lacquer is available in clear form or in color. The advantage of colored lacquer is that it's readily visible as the stencil image is being delineated on the screen. Most lacquers dry rapidly, usually within a matter of ten or fifteen minutes. A well made lacquer blockout stencil (sized or unsized) can last for thousands of impressions and can be used repeatedly for re-runs.

Stencils made with lacquer applied to *unsized screens* can be printed with a wide variety of ink formulations, including tempera paints. In fact, these lacquer stencils can be used with any screen ink except those containing lacquer thinner. Stencils made with *sized screens* can't be printed with inks containing water, for obviously the presence of water will ultimately attack the glue sizing, thus ruining the stencil.

The solvent and thinning agent for lacquer is familiarly known as lacquer thinner. To reclaim an unsized, lacquer blockout screen, lacquer thinner is applied to both sides of the screen until all evidence of lacquer disappears. To reclaim a sized screen, water will do the trick if applied to the underside of the screen. Any stubborn lacquer spots will come off with lacquer thinner applied to both sides.

An important point to remember: lacquer thinner must be used with caution since it's both toxic and inflammable.

Shellac: It doesn't rank among the popular blockout media; one of the main reasons is that when applied to unsized screens, shellac is difficult to wash out. It also seems to have chemical peculiarities which make drying time unpredictable. On certain days it will be bone dry within thirty minutes, and on other days it may take hours, depending to a great extent on the humidity in the air.

Shellac blockout stencils can be used with any printing inks which don't contain alcohol—alcohol being the solvent for shellac. Shellac stencils, sized or unsized, will last for several thousand impressions. As in the reclaiming of lacquer blockout stencils of sized screens, shellac stencils, too, when made on sized screens, can be reclaimed with a water wash applied to the underside to dissolve the glue sizing.

Other blockout media: Principal among these media are polyurethane, varnish, and caustic resist enamels. These are, for the most part, reserved for stencils on screens that aren't intended to be reclaimed. In the textile screen industry where large runs are planned, stencils are often made with no intention of ever reclaiming the screen for re-use on new designs. They're, for every practical purpose, permanent additions to the stock of stencils that are in reserve for repeat orders. Once caustic resist enamels, polyurethane, or varnish have been applied directly to unsized screens, it's almost impossible to remove the design image, regardless of the solvent used.

There's very little likelihood that you'll ever want to prepare a blockout stencil of such permanence, but if you do, it's good to know that these media are available. Your supplier will give you more information about them upon request.

Experimental Improvisations

Blockout stencils can be used not merely to duplicate a graphic image, but also to create an original one. No other stencil method, with the possible exception of the tusche resist method, permits the wide range of improvisations both in texture and design treatments. Indeed, the blockout stencil method can be considered more of a versatile tool to *develop* a design image rather than merely to reproduce one. In some instances, less than a rough sketch—a mere mental image—can serve as a nucleus for a design. This design can evolve extemporaneously during the process of stencil preparation and the application of color.

The blockout compound, whatever it may be— glue, lacquer, shellac, etc.—can be applied to the screen not only by using brushes and other art tools in the conventional manner, but by spattering or dribbling techniques as well. Infinite effects can be obtained by dabbing with sponges, burlap, crushed paper, carpet swatches, and a variety of other texture producing materials.

Essentially, the same tools and techniques can be used creatively in a subtractive manner. First by applying the blockout compound to the screen, then partially removing the compound by pressing against it, some of the compound pulls aways to create interesting textures and effects.

Another way you can achieve novel (and sometimes unpredictable) results is through the use of a partial resist technique. Wet a selected area of the screen with an oily substance, such as mineral spirits or thin machine oil, and then dab a water-glue mixture over it with a sponge. The natural antipathy between oil and water causes the glue to crawl on the screen, resulting in a variety of mosaic effects not easily achievable by any other means.

Blue Butterfly *by Fletcher Martin, courtesy Associated American Artists, New York. This print emphasizing line and texture was produced with tusche and blockout stencils from an original sketch by the artist.*

CHAPTER FIVE

Tusche and other resist stencil methods

To form a better concept of the resist method of stencil preparation, let's compare it with the technique traditionally associated with Javanese batik art in producing hand decorated fabrics.

In batik, the design image is painted on the cloth with liquified wax and allowed to set; after the wax dries the cloth is subjected to a dye solution. Later, when the wax is melted away, the design emerges in the original color of the cloth. The wax has acted as a temporary resist, preventing the dye from reaching selected areas of the cloth.

Tusche, the prime medium employed in the so-called tusche-glue method of stencil preparation, serves a purpose somewhat similar to the wax resist compound employed in batik. To make a tusche-glue stencil, the design to be reproduced is painted or drawn on the surface of the screen with lithographic tusche, a black, slightly greasy compound manufactured in liquid or crayon form. After the design is filled in with tusche, a coat of glue is spread over the entire surface of the screen (design and all), and the glue is allowed to dry. When kerosene or other tusche solvent is applied to the screen, the tusche dissolves, but the glue isn't affected. Whatever residual glue happens to be directly over the tusche (now having nothing to support it) falls off, creating a clearly defined stencil image. The printed result is a facsimile reproduction of the original *tusched-in* image on the screen.

A Comparison of Tusche Resist and Blockout Methods

The tusche method of stencil preparation, like the blockout method previously described, has exceptional possibilities as a creative as well as reproductive art medium. It permits great freedom and spontaneity in the formation of the design image. The artist may choose to work from meticulously rendered art or, if he's venturesome, he may work from a mere sketch. Unlike the blockout method, tusche is a *positive* rather than a negative method. The stencil image is created not by painting *around* the design, but rather by painting the design *itself.* The tusched image, as it appears on the screen is, in a manner of speaking, a preview of the positive design image as it will appear in the print. Every tusche stroke on the screen is a latent stroke on the print.

Prints made with tusche or other resist stencils don't compare in hard-edge sharpness of line with those produced from some of the other stencil making methods. That, in part, explains why resist stencils are rarely used in advertising reproduction. However, for many years the tusche resist method of stencil preparation has been one of the more popular methods of making fine art prints. It's also employed, in a limited way, commercially for textile and wallpaper work, where a personalized, hand-painted effect is desired.

Resist stencils, using glue as a blockout fluid, are intended primarily for limited editions. Where more extended editions are needed, more durable compounds such as lacquer, shellac, or caustic enamel may be used instead of glue.

Basic Materials You'll Need

To make a stencil with the tusche-glue method, you'll need water-soluble glue (the same type as for the blockout method), a small bottle of tusche, and a can of kerosene. You'll also need a good supply of absorbent rags, a strip or two of cardboard, and other incidentals. If you want to experiment with crayon effects, you'll need a few tusche crayons. These crayons are available in both stick or pencil form.

You can make use of your regular kit of art tools: watercolor brushes, lettering brushes, ruling pens, ink compasses, rulers, triangles, and any other tool or device you would normally use to create the original design on paper.

There are a number of modifications of the tusche method of stencil preparation. These modifications depend on the anticipated size of the edition, the nature of the art work, and above all on your personal preferences that are the outgrowth of direct experience with the medium. The basic tusche method, however, employs glue as the blockout fluid. It's the one commonly preferred by artists and printmakers, and is considered most responsive to individual treatments.

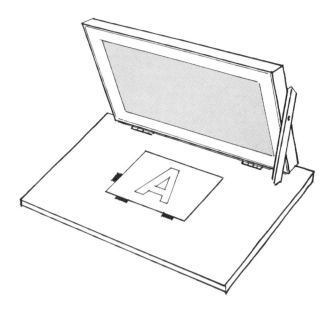

Positioning the artwork in the register guides.

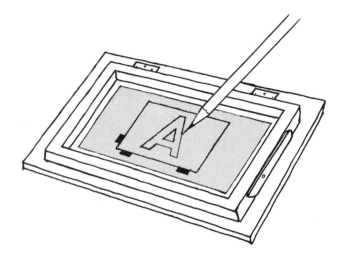

Tracing the design on the screen fabric.

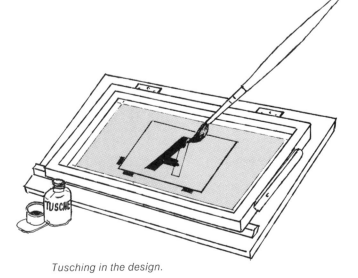

Tusching in the design.

Making a Tusche-Glue Resist Stencil

A suggested procedure follows for making a tusche-glue resist stencil.

Step 1. Position the art on the bed and set the register guides: As in the blockout method previously described, place the art in a horizontal position on the printing bed. Center it visually under the screen, and affix the register guides.

Step 2. Set up for painting in the tusche design: Lower the screen, but keep it from touching the surface below by propping up the front end about ½″ or less.

The art may be left in position on the bed if it's covered with a sheet of transparent acetate. The acetate sheet protects it against the possibility of smudging during the several steps that follow. If you prefer, the art may be traced on the screen with pencil or ink, and then removed.

Stir the tusche well. If it's too thick to work with, add a few drops of water; if it's too free flowing and runny, place a quantity on a blotter to absorb the excess water. Use the blotter as a working palette.

Step 3. Tusche in the design: With a watercolor brush, lettering brush, or other art tool best suited for the particular job, proceed to fill in the design on the screen with the tusche. Make all design areas (whether they're solids, lines, or mere dots) as opaque as possible. Tusche cannot be thinned down to a flow-wash consistency with the hope of achieving a similar effect in the print. If the tusche isn't completely opaque, the blockout fluid will penetrate it, and that portion of the design won't open up in the stencil.

Allow the tusche to dry. This should take thirty to forty minutes. (Actually tusche never "dries"; it merely sets, always retaining its moist, waxy character.) With the design tusched in, the art can be removed from the bed.

Step 4. Check the screen for opacity of tusche application: Hold the screen against a source of light; in this way you can better detect any weak spots in the tusched areas. Retouch with tusche where required. For a perfect stencil, tusche must be fully embedded within the screen mesh, otherwise it won't offer maximum resistance to the glue.

Step 5. Set up for gluing: Mix the glue solution in the proportion of approximately two parts full strength glue to three parts cold or warm water. A cup of mixed glue is more than enough to cover a screen area 20″ x 30″. The leftover glue can be used on another stencil.

Prop up the screen an inch or so above the surface of the bed. The screen must be raised high enough so that the fabric will not touch the surface below during the gluing; yet it should not be elevated at so steep an angle that the glue dribbles or drains off at one end. No glue must reach the underside of the tusched-in areas.

Step 6. Apply the glue coating: Pour a quantity of glue into one side of the screen. With a sharp-edged piece of rigid cardboard, held in the manner of a squeegee, pass the glue evenly across the entire surface of the screen. Go right over the tusched design area. If the cardboard is large enough, it's possible (and desirable) to cover the screen surface with one scrape. Allow the glue to set for five or ten minutes.

Follow with a second coat applied the same way. Then, with a small piece of cardboard, scoop up the excess glue around edges and corners of the screen, and place it back in the container.

Allow the glue coating to dry thoroughly. With the aid of a fan, the glue should dry within twenty-five to thirty minutes; otherwise it may take the better part of an hour.

Examine the screen by holding it against a light. If there are a few isolated pinholes, they can be touched up with a dab of glue; if they're widespread, it would indicate that an additional coat is necessary. Be sure that the glue coating is bone dry before you proceed with the next step, which is to dissolve the tusched areas.

Step 7. Dissolve the tusched design image: Dissolving the tusche may be done on the printing bed, or preferably, on a work table. Either way, spread several large sheets of newspaper directly under the screen. Pour a liberal amount of kerosene (or any of the petroleum or mineral spirit solvents) into the screen. With a rag, swish it around, rubbing over the tusched areas. The kerosene dissolves the tusche but not the glue.

Replace newspaper sheets as they become supersaturated with kerosene and dissolved tusche. Next rub down the underside of the screen with kerosene. As the tusche dissolves, whatever residual glue rests over it flakes off. The stencil image of the design emerges in clear unobstructed mesh when all the tusche is gone. Finish with a dry cloth rubdown on both sides of the screen.

Step 8. Check the screen: Once more, holding the screen up against a light, check to see if the design image is completely open. Isolated particles of glue trapped within the design image can be dislodged by gently rubbing with a fingernail or suede brush.

Touch up any pinholes in the glue which may have developed in the process of dissolving the tusche. When that's done, the stencil is ready for ink and squeegee.

The Sized Screen Method

A variation in the procedure just outlined is to size the screen with a cornstarch solution prior to *tusching in* the design. The sizing temporarily closes the mesh, thus minimizing the possibility of tusche seeping through the screen. It also provides a smoother working surface for applying the tusche and makes for somewhat sharper printing.

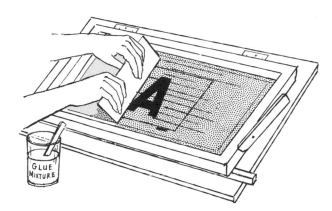
Coating the screen with the glue mixture.

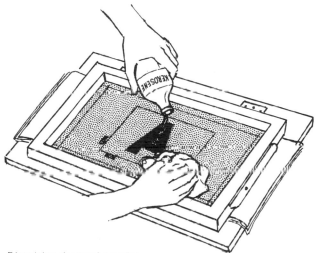
Dissolving the tusche resist.

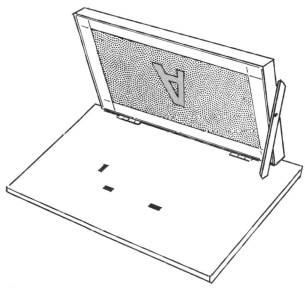
Stencil ready for printing.

Briefly, here are the steps necessary to prepare a resist stencil with a sized screen.

Step 1: Make a pencil or ball point outline tracing of the design on the screen.

Step 2: Prepare the sizing. This is done by dissolving a heaping tablespoon of cornstarch in a glass of lukewarm water.

Step 3: With a sponge, large camel's hair brush, or wad of absorbent cotton, spread an even coat of the sizing solution on the underside of the screen. (If sizing is applied to the upper surface of the screen, the water in the sizing may wash away the tracing.)

Step 4: Allow the sizing to dry. The sizing forms a chalk-like surface coating which will automatically come off at a later stage when the tusche is washed out.

From here on, the basic procedure (already given) for tusching, gluing, washing out, etc., is followed.

Textures

Compared to the blockout method, the resist method offers even greater latitude in achieving textural treatments and configurations. In addition to dry-brush, stippling, spatter, and crosshatching, a variety of other textural effects can be produced by dabbing liquid resist onto the screen. Sponges, crumpled wax paper, swatches of carpet, and "found" objects of every description can be used to dab on the tusche. Variations in texture are further extended by the use of tusche in crayon form. Tusche crayons produce soft, sketchy lines which have a charcoal or pastel-like quality. By placing material with textured surfaces (such as sandpaper, Rossboard, mosquito netting, leather, canvas, burlap, etc.) under the screen, and rubbing the tusche crayon over it, a pattern impression of the textured material will result. In the rubbing technique, you must bear down on the screen surface hard enough for the tusche to embed itself into the mesh, yet not so hard as to damage the screen fabric.

Resists

Theoretically, any film forming substance can serve as a resist medium, provided the solvent used to dissolve the resist doesn't also dissolve the blockout medium. Thus, lacquer (which dissolves with lacquer thinner) may be used as a resist if glue (which dissolves with water) is used as a blockout. Or the roles may be reversed; glue may serve as a resist if lacquer is the blockout. In actual practice, however, the best resists, by far, are those especially formulated for the purpose. These include lithographic tusche, liquid wax, and a latex composition commercially identified as *liquid frisket*. The latter, however, is in a category by itself.

Tusche: This is the most versatile of the resist compounds, and the one most frequently used by artists. It comes in liquid and crayon form. Liquid tusche is used for solids, line work, stipple, crosshatching, and other art techniques and handles as easily as poster colors. Diluted to the proper consistency, it's adaptable for use with a ruling pen and compass. Liquid tusche is put up in 2-oz., 4-oz., and half-pint bottles and has a long shelf life.

In its liquid state, tusche resembles black India ink, but has a slightly waxy feel to it. Chemically, it's composed of stearic acid, lamp black or nigrosine, and a wax compound such as tallow. When wet, tusche is soluble in water; when dry, it's soluble in kerosene, naphtha, benzine, turpentine, or any of the mineral or petroleum spirits; kerosene is the least inflammable and the least expensive spirit.

Tusche, in crayon form, is used mainly for textures, rubbings, and charcoal technique effects. It comes in grades from #0, very soft, to #5, extra hard; #2 in generally considered medium.

Among the better known brands of tusche used in screen stencil preparation, as well as in lithography, is Korn's, found at leading graphic art suppliers.

Wax resist: This is a water-soluble resist employed frequently to prepare stencils which are used with emulsion dyes for printing on fabrics. However, there's no reason why it can't have wider application for general printing purposes as well.

Wax resist is formulated to be used cold in liquid form. It solidifies after it has been applied to the screen. It's an easy, inexpensive medium to use.

The design is painted on the screen in the usual manner. When the wax solidifies, the surface of the screen is coated with enamel, lacquer, shellac, or other waterproof blockout compound. After the coating is completely dry (drying time varies with the nature of the compound), both sides of the screen are washed with hot water. The wax dissolves, and in so doing, opens up the stencil image leaving the waterproof blockout compound around it.

Liquid frisket: Sold under such trade names as *Art Maskoid* and *E-Z Liquid Frisket,* this type of resist is a fluid latex composition; upon drying, it congeals somewhat like rubber cement.

The stencil image is produced on the screen by applying the latex resist with brush, pen or other art tools—the same as when applying liquid tusche. The screen is then given a coating of blockout fluid. (This may be glue, lacquer, shellac, or other compound.) Up to this point, the procedure is identical for both methods. The manner in which these resists are removed from the screen, however, differs radically. Whereas tusche requires a solvent that will not affect its surrounding blockout medium, no solvent is needed to remove the latex resist. Once dry, the frisket comes off the screen by rubbing it with a square of crepe rubber eraser thus opening the design image of the stencil.

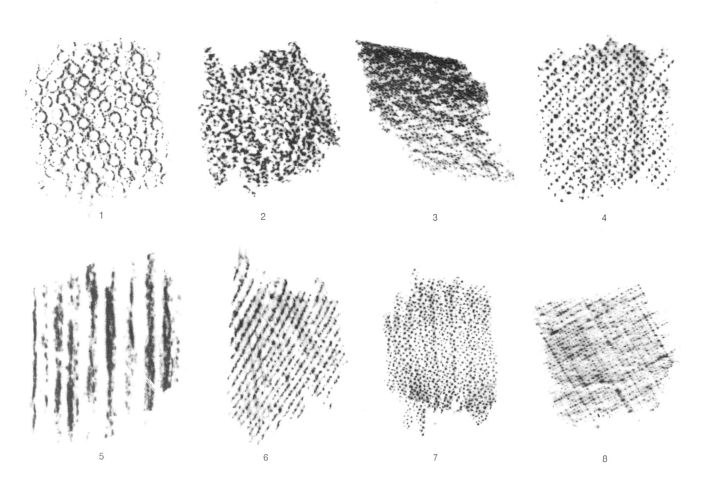

TEXTURAL TREATMENTS

1. Metal wire screen
2. Sandpaper
3. Grained matboard
4. Back of Masonite
5. Wood (face)
6. Wood (end grain)
7. Rossboard
8. Linen
9. Stipple with sponge
10. Drybrush
11. Crosshatch with brush
12. Spatter

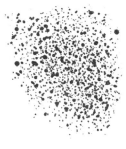

A wide almost infinite variety of textural treatments are possible with the resist stencil method.

Those who show a preference for latex resist over the tusche resist method claim for it a number of advantages. It's considerably more opaque than tusche and, therefore, requires a minimum of touching up; no inflammable solvents are needed. Liquid frisket doesn't stain the fabric as tusche sometimes does—a condition which shows up when the screen is reclaimed. Then too, since removing the resist does not entail working with fluids, this phase of stencil preparation—according to its adherents—is "less messy."

Because latex resist can be used only in liquid form, some of the textural nuances and rubbing techniques possible with tusche crayons cannot be as easily introduced into the design image.

Consistency of Blockout Fluids

Generally speaking, glue or any other blockout compound, used as a *coating* for a resist screen, works

With tusche (in liquid or crayon form) it's possible to retain the character of the original sketch.

best when diluted to about the consistency of maple syrup. The consistency, however, may be varied with regard to both the nature of the design to be reproduced, and the extent of the intended edition. Designs with delicate line work and subtle textures wash out more easily when the blockout is somewhat thinner, but the resist stencil will be less durable. Large masses and solids can safely stand a heavier coat. Judgment in the matter of consistency will come with experience.

Applying the Coating

When applying the coating, it's best to keep the screen in a fairly level position. In this way, the possibility of the blockout fluid running under the resist areas is diminished. Any resist thus trapped wont' wash out. Some printers make it a practice, when coating a screen, to unhook it from its hinges, and place it in a level position supported on two strips of wood or across two saw horses.

For a smooth, uniform coating, check to be sure that the edge of the scrape card is cut sharp. A rough edge will cause ridges in the coating—a condition which retards the drying, makes washing out the resist difficult, and tends to damage the squeegee rubber when printing. Commercial scrapers made of plastic or aluminum are available.

When using a cardboard (or commercial) scraper, pass the blockout fluid from one side of the screen to the other. Use one, even-pressured sweep without stopping along the way. Avoid repeating or overlapping strokes. When applying more than one coat (a common practice), wait for the first coat to set or dry before applying the next.

Washing Out Tusche

When washing out the tusche resist, there's no harm in letting the kerosene soak into the image area for twenty to thirty minutes (or even longer). The more saturated the tusche gets, the easier it will come out, and the better the final stencil will be. For extended soaking, kerosene is better than benzine, naphtha, turpentine, or some of the other mineral spirits. It's the least volatile and, therefore, will remain wet the longest.

Reclaiming the Screen

Screens made with the resist method, when no longer needed, may be reclaimed in the same way as those made by the blockout method. In each case, the washing solvent used to remove the stencil image must be compatible with the blockout medium; for example if glue is the blockout medium, then water will be the washing solvent; if lacquer is the blockout medium, the washing solvent will be lacquer thinner, etc.

Reclining Nude by Fay Lansner, courtesy Steve Poleskie, New York. The tusche-resist method lends itself amiably to contour drawings such as the one shown here reproduced with three coordinated color stencils.

(Above) The Black Fish *by Harry Krug, courtesy Associated American Artists, New York. A subtle balance between textural treatment and depth of color characterizes this limited edition screen print.*

(Left) Steve and Liza *by Raphael Soyer, 24" x 36", edition —40, courtesy Steve Poleskie, New York. Tusche in crayon form was the prime resist medium used to reproduce this sensitive drawing by this well known artist.*

CHAPTER SIX

The paper stencil method

In theory, cutting paper stencils is as simple as cutting out paper dolls. Fundamentally, making a paper stencil involves tracecutting the design on a sheet of paper, and placing it on the printing bed; then pulling an impression to adhere the stencil to the screen. The natural viscosity of the ink used in screen printing is sufficient to adhere the paper to the screen. When the paper segments corresponding to the design image are stripped from the screen, the stencil is ready for printing.

Making A Paper Stencil

Step 1. Position the art on the bed: Place the art in a horizontal position on the printing bed, centering it visually under the screen; affix the register guides.

Step 2. Secure the stencil paper onto the art: With the screen in a raised position, tape a sheet of transparent paper over the art. The paper should be cut to size, ½" or so larger than the inside dimensions of the screen. This eliminates the need for masking out the area between screen frame and stencil image.

Tracing paper, vellum, newsprint, bond, or for that matter, any thin white paper is acceptable, provided that it's fairly transparent, lies flat, and is free from wrinkles or creases. The best paper for this purpose is white transparent sign paper; this is the kind sign painters use for window streamers. It comes in rolls and sheets.

Step 3. Cut the stencil: Carefully tracecut outlines of the art as you see them through the paper using a well sharpened stencil knife. Bear down with just enough pressure to cut through the paper. Leave all cut areas in place.

Step 4. Code the cut parts: For easy identification, place an x (or other symbol) on all segments of the paper stencil corresponding to the printing areas. (These segments are stripped away after the stencil is adhered to the screen.)

Step 5. Release the paper stencil from the art: Carefully remove the tape that holds the stencil sheet to the art. Avoid any motion which might ruffle or shift the sheet causing the segments to move out of position. Then, lower the screen.

Step 6. Adhere the stencil: Pour a liberal quantity of printing ink onto the center of the screen and with a firm and even pressure, squeegee it from the center outward to both sides. Then, squeegee across once or twice to be sure that the ink penetrates the screen and completely covers the stencil sheet below. This action also removes air pockets. You needn't worry about getting an impression on the art. At this stage, the entire screen area is still blocked out by the as-yet-unopened stencil.

Step 7. Strip the stencil: Raise the screen, but not so high as to cause the squeegee and ink to drop out. The stencil sheet now clings firmly to the underside of the screen. To prevent the stencil from shifting, and as a safeguard against leakage, place several small strips of tape around the edges of the stencil sheet.

Pull away all stencil segments identified with the x mark. These are clearly discernible if the screen is viewed against a source of light. The art may now be removed from the bed, and you are ready for printing.

Advantages and Limitations of the Paper Stencil

The paper stencil method has a number of distinct advantages. In some ways, it's the simplest of all stencil making techniques. Minutes after the stencil is cut, it's ready for printing. The stencil adheres itself with the first passing of the squeegee. Since the stencil sheet can easily be made large enough to cover the entire screen area, there's no additional masking out to do. It's also the least expensive of all stencil making methods; the cost of paper is negligible. Also, there are no special removing fluids, adherents or commercial masking-out compounds to purchase.

Prints made with paper stencils are characterized by literally knife-cut sharpness. It's much easier to get an incised, built-up effect with paper stencils than with any other stencil technique.

There are some inherent limitations. A paper stencil can only be used once; it can't be saved for a re-run. The printing must be done at one time; it can't be carried over to the next day. Then too, a

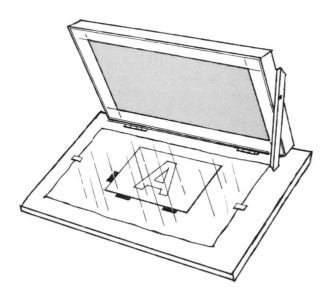

Positioning the stencil paper over the artwork set in the register guides.

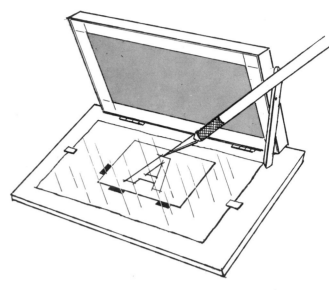

Tracecutting design outlines.

Squeegeeing ink across the screen to adhere the paper stencil.

Stripping the stencil to open the printing areas.

paper stencil lacks the durability of stencils made by other methods; it's not recommended for printing editions that extend beyond 100 to 150 impressions, at most. After a while, the stencil tends to become oversaturated with ink, diminishing its further usefulness. Another drawback: there's practically no margin for error in mixing the ink. When printing with paper stencils, the ink must be right from the very start. Once the printing is under way, there's very little opportunity to make adjustments. If the ink proves to be too thick (or too quick drying), thus clogging the mesh, it then becomes necessary to wash and wipe the mesh. Thus, the stencil sheet stands a good chance of being ruined. If the ink is too thin, it lacks the proper viscosity and holding power; consequently parts of the stencil are apt to shift out of position or drop off entirely.

All in all, the paper stencil method is best suited for projects where the work to be reproduced consists of fair sized lettering and simple massive shapes, and where the editions are restricted to short runs.

The Mimeograph Paper Stencil Technique

Though limited in commercial application, mimeograph stencils can be used with screen printing for short-run editions. With this mimeograph stencil you can reproduce typewritten copy, line drawings, and whatever else is reproducible by the standard mimeograph process.

Here, in essence, is how the mimeograph technique can be combined with screen printing. The mimeograph stencil sheet, the identical kind used for office mimeograph machines, is typed or drawn in exactly the same way as if it were being prepared for mimeographing. A mimeograph stencil sheet, as you may know, consists of a surface layer of a chemically bonded carbon compound supported on a highly tensile, but porous, paper tissue. Through the impact of typewriter keys, or by means of a ball point pen or stylus, the carbon surface is removed. The removal of this surface exposes the porous tissue through which a fluid ink can penetrate. The mimeograph stencil sheet (carbon side up) is placed on a cardboard and positioned on the printing bed. Then, a paper mask is cut to block out the open area between the stencil and the screen frame. The screen is lowered, and ink squeegeed across. When the screen is lifted, the stencil sheet and paper mask cling to the underside of the screen. In the course of printing, the ink flows easily through the open parts of the porous tissue, but doesn't go through the parts covered by the layer of carbon.

A stencil of this kind is good for an edition of up to 100 or thereabouts; beyond that amount, the stencil image begins to blur and disintegrate.

Cutting Tools

There are no standard cutting tools strictly reserved for cutting paper stencils. It's mostly a matter of

An easy-to-render freehand alphabet, such as the one shown here, is especially suited for the paper stencil method. There are no "island" parts to shift out of position or drop out.

Interesting negative image effects can be achieved by pasting pre-cut gummed paper to the underside of the open screen area. Courtesy The American Crayon Co., New Jersey.

Metropolis *by Jane Kosarin, courtesy the High School of Art and Design, New York. The artist, a student of the Screen Print Workshop at the High School of Art and Design, used three stencils to produce this print: the rectangular areas within the outline superstructure were printed with paper stencils; the superstructure was printed with a handcut film stencil.*

personal preference. The prevalent practice in the trade is to use a small angular shaped cutting blade locked in a pencil shaped holder. Some prefer working with an X-Acto knife which comes equipped with a set of removable blades of different sizes and shapes. Others are accustomed to working with single edge razor blades which have the advantage of being disposable. Whatever cutting tool is used, it's very important that it be razor sharp. A smooth, honing stone must be made available for tools which require sharpening.

For mechanically produced circles, a compass may be employed if the pencil part is replaced with a well sharpened stylus.

Cutting the Stencil

To avoid marring the original art in the process of cutting the stencil, you can cut the stencil from a pencil tracing. In fact, the tracing itself can serve as the stencil and be adhered to the screen. Another practical suggestion is to place a sheet of acetate between the art and the stencil paper. This not only will protect the art, but it also will provide a smoother undersurface to work on.

If you find that the stencil paper isn't transparent enough to see through clearly, a little kerosene, turpentine, or oil applied to the surface will improve its transparency.

Usually, intersecting lines or overcuts in the paper stencil don't show up in the print. Nonetheless, it's good practice to keep overcuts down to a minimum, and make them as short as possible.

After completing the cutting, it's important to make a final check to assure that all printing areas are cut. Once the stencil sheet is adhered to the screen, it's frustrating to come upon some printing elements which either have been forgotten, or else not cut through sufficiently to peel off the screen.

It's sometimes advisable to leave one or two *uncut* nicks strategically placed within each printing area of the paper stencil. This will keep the elements from shifting out of position before adhering. After the stencil sheet is adhered to the screen, it will not be difficult to break the tiny nicks when stripping the stencil.

Adhering the Stencil

Here's a precautionary measure to prevent isolated centers from shifting or dropping off during printing. Prior to adhering (with the screen resting on the cut stencil), place a spot of glue on the surface of the screen fabric, directly over each of the centers. The glue, as it seeps through the screen and dries, will keep the centers anchored to it.

Printing

To get a heavier deposit of ink, where an impasto effect is desired, select a heavier paper for the stencil. The thickness of the ink deposit is determined mostly by the thickness of the stencil sheet. Other determining factors are the size of the screen mesh, the viscosity of the ink, and the amount of squeegee pressure.

Almost any kind of screen ink can be employed when printing with paper stencils, as long as it doesn't contain water; water tends to wrinkle and distort the paper.

Although paper stencils are designed for hard-edge printing, some textural variations are possible. Tearing or singeing the paper's edges will produce novel effects interesting to those who use the paper stencil method experimentally, as a creative art medium. Simulated tonal effects (often unpredictable) are also possible with the use of rice paper and other substances with varying degrees of porosity. The amount of ink seeping through is determined by the degree of porosity of the paper.

Reclaiming the Screen

Of all stencil making methods, screens used with paper stencils are easiest and fastest to reclaim. No solvents are needed. To clear the screen, and free it from the stencil image, simply peel off the paper clinging to the underside of the screen. This paper comes off almost automatically when the printing ink is scooped up at the end of the edition and the screen is washed. Any spot of glue used to anchor the isolated parts of the stencil will come off with water. The screen, itself, is in no way impaired by the paper stencil tissue.

The stencil knife shown here is one of·many that can be used for cutting paper stencils. It features a removable blade.

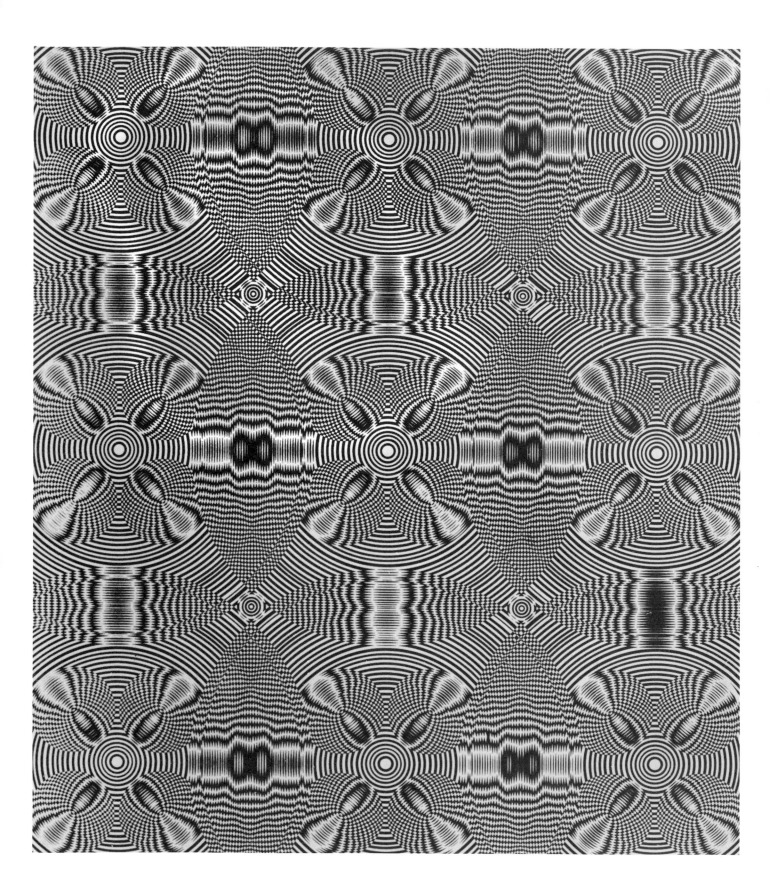

Whirlwind *by Lou Bonderoff, 20″ x 24″, courtesy the artist. This highly intricate design was produced with a film stencil cut entirely by hand with the aid of a compass equipped with a small blade attachment.*

CHAPTER SEVEN

The film stencil method

This method is reserved for work where a sharp line and precise detail are essential to the quality of a print. Like the paper stencil method, the film method is capable of reproducing design elements and lettering with razor-edged sharpness. Yet the more flexible nature of the stencil film allows for infinitely greater detail than is possible with the paper stencil. A well made film stencil practically never wears out. It can be used for many thousands of prints without loss of quality or character.

The film stencil method has long been one of the favorite methods employed by commercial screen printers. Its potential as a fine art medium, however, has only recently been fully recognized and exploited.

Making a Film Stencil

The basic blockout medium for the film stencil method is a transparent laminated film which consists of two layers. The upper layer is composed of a lacquer, or a water-soluble emulsion, which serves as the stencil tissue; a lower layer of glassine paper, or a plastic material such as Mylar, serves as a backing sheet. In creating the stencil image, it's the upper layer only that's cut and stripped away; the backing sheet remains intact. The backing sheet merely acts as a temporary carrier for the cut stencil until it's adhered to the screen.

Here's the procedure in greater detail.

Step 1. Tape the film over the art: Measure off a sheet of stencil film, cutting it several inches larger all around than the art. Center it (emulsion side up) over the art and tape it down with several pieces of masking tape.

The design to be reproduced may be merely an outline working drawing, or it may be rendered in a more comprehensive or finished technique. In cutting the stencil, we're concerned with boundaries or outlines only. It makes little difference whether they're filled in or left as lines.

Step 2. Cut the design image: With the tip of a small bladed stencil knife, tracecut the outlines of the design that you see through the film. Hold the knife per-

pendicular to the surface of the film sheet. Press lightly enough to cut through the upper layer without penetrating the backing sheet. This may seem a bit difficult at first, but it won't take long before you acquire the proper feel to know how much— or rather, how little—pressure to apply. If the stencil knife is in good condition, the little blade will glide along with ease, following straight lines, round lines, and around corners, leaving a clean, incised outline-tracing in its wake.

A ruler, celluloid triangle, or other straight edge can be used as a mechanical guide to cut straight lines. A compass with a blade attachment will cut circles with one twirl of the instrument.

Don't worry about intersecting overcuts, because they automatically close up when the stencil is adhered to the screen. Overcuts in film stencils don't show up in the print. When the design is completely tracecut, the stencil is ready for stripping.

Step 3. Strip the film: Place the tip of the stencil blade at any intersecting point of the area to be stripped. With that as a start, pull upward a little, just enough to get a good finger grip. The rest is easy. The cut areas strip away without resistance. By the way, remember that the areas you strip are those that show up in the print. They become the *open* parts of the stencil. The areas left in film become the *closed* parts of the stencil.

Check the stencil to see that you've cut and stripped away all the film you're supposed to. Remove any stray piece of film or speck of dirt that may be on the film tissue. After the stencil has been adhered, it's bothersome—at times almost impossible—to dislodge any foreign matter without impairing the quality of the stencil.

Step 4. Set the guides: Position the art (with film still attached) on the printing bed so that the stencil area is visually centered under the screen. Staple or tape it down temporarily.

As usual, fasten three register guides on the bed; one goes flush against the lower left side of the art; the other two go along the bottom.

Step 5. Adhere the film: A few preliminary steps precede the actual adhering. First, check to see that

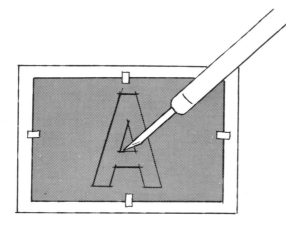

Tracecutting the design outlines on the film.

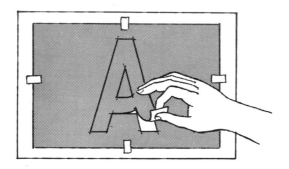

Stripping the film.

Positioning the stripped film in the register guides, ready for adhering.

the screen fabric is immaculately clean, free from dirt or grease. Then remove most of the tape that holds the film to the art, leaving two small pieces. These will be enough to keep the film from shifting during adhering. Finally, lower the screen, making sure that fabric and film are in perfect contact.

☐ *Adhering lacquer film stencils*—The adhering fluid is a species of lacquer thinner; it's specifically formulated to serve as an adhering agent for the film being used. It can usually be purchased from the manufacturer of the film.

Saturate a small cloth with adhering fluid. Wring it out so that it's damp, and not dripping wet. With one hand, apply the damp cloth lightly to the surface of the screen directly over the film area, covering a small section at a time. With the other hand, follow immediately with a brisk rubdown with a dry cloth. Continue this wetting and drying procedure until the entire stencil area is adhered. A fan helps to quickly evaporate any trace of adhering fluid lingering within the screen mesh. The screen should normally dry within ten or fifteen minutes. When the adhering fluid seeps through the mesh and reaches the film, it softens tne film just enough to make it stick to the screen. When this happens, the film takes on a deeper hue. The rubdown removes the excess fluid, and reinforces and completes the adhesion.

☐ *Adhering water-soluble film stencils*—Here the adhering fluid is prepared by the user. It consists of one part 99% isopropyl alcohol mixed with three parts water.

Using a generous amount of this alcohol-water adherent, apply it to the film area of the screen with a soft cloth. Wet a 6″ or 8″ section at a time. Blot the section immediately with white newsprint paper. The blotting action removes excess adherent, and, at the same time, presses the film firmly to the screen. Continue this wetting-blotting procedure until the entire film is adhered. Allow forty minutes or thereabouts for the screen to dry thoroughly.

Some manufacturers of water-soluble stencil film recommend an alcohol-vinegar adherent made up of one part 99% isopropyl alcohol and two parts white vinegar.

Step 6. Remove the backing sheet: When the stencil image is thoroughly dry, raise the screen. You'll note that the film has pulled itself completely away from the art, and now clings tenaciously to the underside of the screen.

Are you ready for printing? Not quite yet. First the backing sheet has to be removed. Start by lifting one corner of the sheet; once that's done, the rest will peel off easily, usually in one piece. The removal of the backing sheet opens the stencil.

Step 7. Mask out the screen area surrounding the stencil tissue: As a matter of economy, stencil film is hardly ever cut large enough to cover the entire screen area. The open space on the screen between film and frame must, therefore, be masked out. To do this first raise the screen an inch or so to make sure that the screen fabric is not in contact with the bed. Then with a sharp-edged piece of cardboard or a commercial scraper, apply an even coat of lacquer, glue, or other mask-out medium to the open screen area. Slightly overlap the maskout medium onto the margin of the film, and then allow it to dry.

The screen may also be masked-out from the underside by removing it from the hinges and placing it upside down on a flat work table.

Step 8. Check the stencil: Touch up any leaks or pinholes that may appear either on the film tissue or the surrounding area. The screen is now all set for printing.

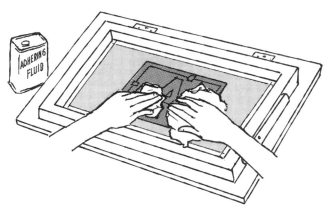

Adhering the film to the screen.

Tools and Supplies

A wide range of knives and cutters as well as auxiliary equipment is available in many styles to suit both individual preferences and the needs of the job at hand.

Stencil knives: Unlike artists' lettering or watercolor brushes, stencil knives are not categorically classified by size. Generally, one stencil knife is used to cut both large and small areas, the size of the blade bears little relation to the size of the cutting area. There are, however, several different styles of knives available. The choice is a matter of personal preference.

In the main, there are three styles: the fixed blade knife, the interchangeable blade knife, and the swivel blade knife.

☐ *Fixed blade knife*—This is the simplest and perhaps the most common stencil cutting tool used by artists and craftsmen. The blade of tempered steel is permanently attached to a penholder handle of wood or metal.

Peeling off the backing sheet to open the stencil.

☐ *Interchangeable blade knife*—This is similar to the fixed blade knife, except that it comes with a vise-like chuck. This chuck releases the blade so that it can be replaced, or inverted point-side down for protection when not in use.

☐ *Swivel blade knife*—This is a fine, precision tool featuring a blade of surgical steel mounted in a ball-bearing socket. The blade, which rotates freely in any direction with the movement of the hand, enables you to cut graceful curves without twisting the handle. The swivel action can be stopped by turning a knurled nut.

Special cutters: These tools have fairly specialized functions. The three basic types are the dual cutter, the line cutter, and the circle cutter.

☐ *Dual cutter*—This tool has twin blades that cut two parallel lines simultaneously. Its use is somewhat limited, reserved primarily for borders, double outlines, and graphs. Dual cutters come with fixed blades of varying widths as well as adjustable ones.

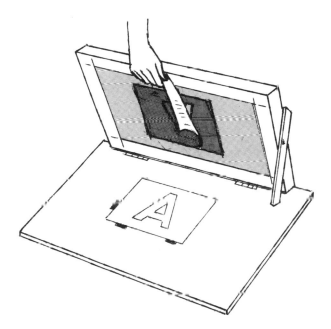

Blocking out the open area of the screen surrounding the film.

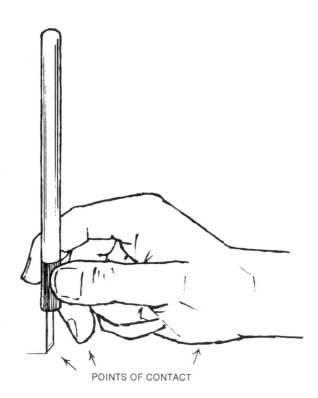

POINTS OF CONTACT

When cutting film, the stencil knife is held lightly between the fingers with just enough pressure to cut through the film surface without penetrating the backing sheet.

☐ *Line cutter*—This has a loop-like blade arrangement that cuts lines and peels out the film all in one stroke. It can be used for certain types of line drawings, crosshatching, and graphs.

☐ *Circle cutter*—There are several types. The bow compass cutter is nothing more than a standard draftsman's compass with a cutting head attachment. It cuts circles ranging from the size of a dot to 12″ in diameter.

Another type works on a beam compass principle. It's made of high quality steel, with both edges of the cutting blade sharpened to permit rotation in either direction (clockwise or counterclockwise). It's intended primarily for cutting small circles with unerring accuracy.

A variation of the beam compass, the Trummel cutter, is specifically designed for cutting very large circles. Usually equipped with a single blade, the Trummel cutter also has a special attachment for a dual blade; this dual blade cuts double concentric circles simultaneously.

Sharpening stone: Normally, the stencil blade keeps its cutting edge for a long time. When it does require a bit of sharpening or honing, a small sharpening stone such as the fine grained Arkansas stone is recommended. To restore the cutting edge more completely, or to remove a nick or burr, a heavier textured oil stone is necessary.

Work lamp: Knife cuts on film aren't easily visible with ordinary overhead illumination. A direct source of light such as that provided by a flexible gooseneck lamp, a fluorescent desk lamp, or a high intensity Tensor-type light is indispensable for precision work in cutting film stencils.

Magnifying glass: For cutting intricate detail, whether it's lettering or design, a magnifying glass will be helpful. There are several kinds on the market. One is meant to be worn on the forehead in the manner of a visor or eyeshade; it permits perfect mobility when working at close range. Another type is a magnifying glass mounted on a stand equipped with a flexible metal arm that easily adjusts to any position. Also available is a table lamp model that combines both a fluorescent light and a magnifier.

Stencil Films

There are three kinds of stencil film: lacquer, water-soluble, and lacquerproof. All come with paper and plastic backing sheets. Plastic backed films are far more popular since they have exceptional transparency. They lie flat and are unaffected by changes in temperature or humidity; they're easy to cut, strip, and adhere.

Lacquer film: The choice of most commercial practitioners in the field, lacquer films have much to recommend them. Stencils made with lacquer film can be used with oil based paints, tempera colors, textile emulsions, enamels, varnish, and glue. In fact,

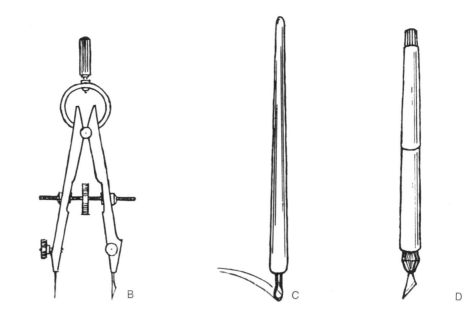

(A) Adjustable in width, this type of stencil knife cuts two parallel lines simultaneously. (B) A bow compass with a small stencil blade attachment cuts mechanically perfect circles. (C) Good for freehand line drawing, ruled line work, and simple contour drawings, this film stencil knife cuts and strips in one operation. (D) This swivel blade stencil knife can cut in all directions, without rotating the handle.

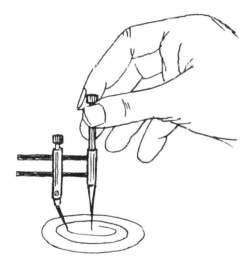

This "beam" type compass is made for cutting small circles.

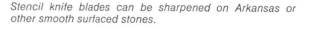

Stencil knife blades can be sharpened on Arkansas or other smooth surfaced stones.

An expansion beam compass cuts large circles.

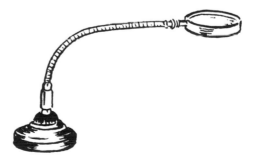

This magnifying glass comes with a flexible neck mounted to a self-supporting base.

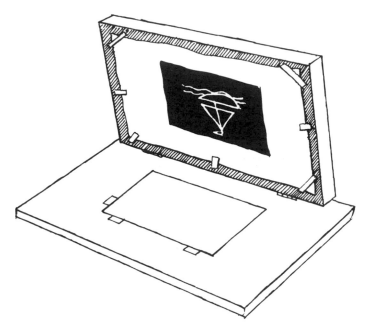

Cut paper (with window opening for stencil area) applied to the underside of the screen serves as an expedient "maskout" for short runs.

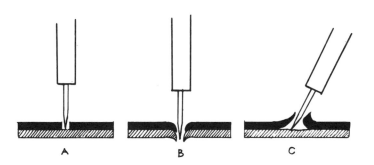

This schematic view demonstrates how the quality of a film cut is affected by the position and pressure of the stencil blade: (A) Good—blade is perpendicular, and the pressure applied is just enough to cut the film without penetrating the backing sheet; (B) Poor—blade is perpendicular, but too much pressure cuts both film and backing sheet; (C) Poor—pressure is right, but blade cuts the film at an angle causing the film surface to lift. Good cutting makes for good adhering.

any printing medium which doesn't contain a lacquer solvent is compatible with lacquer films.

Water-soluble film: While this film can be used with standard oil based paints, it's primarily meant for printing with lacquer inks, acrylics, and vinyls. Water-soluble film possesses an added feature that makes it particularly desirable for home and school use; no chemical solvent is required. Adhering is done with a simple water-alcohol solution which is negligible in cost, offers no fire hazard, and has no noxious odor. The stencil image, when no longer needed, is easily removed with warm water.

Lacquerproof film: Used primarily for printing with decal lacquers, this type of film is especially formulated to resist the biting action of nitrocellulose inks. It comes with special solvents for adhering as well as removing the film tissue.

Stencil films are made in three basic colors: blue, green, and amber. Blue is the most popular, because it least distorts the true color values of the art when viewed through the film. Blue is also the least reflective of the films and therefore easiest on the eyes.

Stencil films are sold under such trade names as Ulano Film, Nu-film, Blu-film, Profilm, Craftint, and Studnite, and are packaged in single sheets and rolls. They're available in three weights: thin, medium, and heavy. Commercial printers like to work with the lightweight film, because it leaves a minimal deposit of ink on the printing surface—something which is regarded with high favor in the trade. Medium and heavyweight films are reserved for jobs where a built-up effect is desired.

Masking-out Media

The masking-out media used to block out the open screen area depend largely on the nature of the stencil and the formulation of the printing ink used.

Lacquer: Any fast-drying lacquer may be used as a masking-out medium to fill in the open mesh, but it's better to use special screen lacquers formulated for the purpose. Screen lacquer (also known as *fill-in* or *blockout* lacquer) is available clear and in color. It can be applied to the screen with a brush. However, scraping the lacquer with a sharp-edged, cardboard or commercial scraper produces a more even coat and is considerably faster. As it comes in the container, lacquer has the consistency of maple syrup. It may be thinned, if necessary, with adhering fluid, film remover, or any of the commercial lacquer solvents.

Glue: A fish-type glue, which retains its water solubility after it dries, makes an excellent masking-out medium. Traditionally, LePage's Full Strength Liquid Glue has been the preferred choice, but it's by no means the only water-soluble glue available for the purpose. Any good grade of glue that dries quickly, doesn't become brittle, and dissolves easily with cold water can be used.

Proprietary blockout compounds: Sold under such varied trade names as Water-Sol, Blox, and Water-mask, these glue-like formulations can be used with lacquer film stencils as well as with all other water resistant stencils. When reclaiming the screen, the compounds can be easily removed with cold water. They're in some ways superior to ordinary glue mixtures, because they dry considerably faster, hold up better, possess excellent flexibility, and remain stable under all weather conditions.

Paper: Instead of using a liquid masking-out medium such as lacquer or glue, the open area surrounding the film tissue may be masked out with paper strips or a large sheet of paper with a window cutout, applied to the underside of the screen. Paper maskouts are adequate for short editions. While practically any kind of flat paper can be used, white newsprint paper, bond paper, and sign writers' window paper are best.

Hints on Cutting and Stripping the Film

To check the cutting edge of the stencil blade, cut a series of closely spaced crosshatch lines on a piece of film. If the blade is sharp, the areas between the intersecting cuts (no matter how small) stay in place; if the blade is dull or has developed a burr, the tiny intersections pop up and drop away. The "crosshatch test" is also a check on the condition of the film. Fresh film will steadfastly hold intersecting areas.

Another way of checking the sharpness of the blade is to cut a series of silhouetted profiles in one or two continuous strokes—doing so without lifting the stencil knife. A blade with a keen edge will glide smoothly along the contours of the profile (front and back) allowing the entire silhouette to be stripped in one piece.

A pair of tweezers comes in handy as an aid in stripping film. Masking tape wound around the finger, with the sticky part out, can be used as a pick-up for stray pieces of film left in open areas.

If an isolated segment of film (for example, the center of a letter) has shifted, dropped out, or has been stripped by error, it can be replaced without difficulty. Either press it down firmly in position with the tip of a finger, or if this is not sufficient to hold it a touch of diluted rubber cement will do the trick.

A sheet of paper or acetate placed under the hand while cutting will help protect the surface of the film from smudges, grease marks, or normal perspiration. Film that's kept clean adheres the easiest.

Hints on Adhering the Film

Trouble-free adhering depends to a great extent on the cleanliness of the screen fabric. This applies to

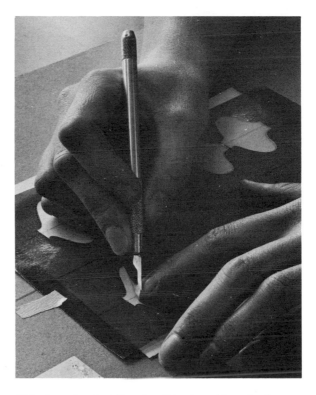

Stripping a handcut film stencil is viewed here in closeup. Photo courtesy The American Crayon Co., New Jersey.

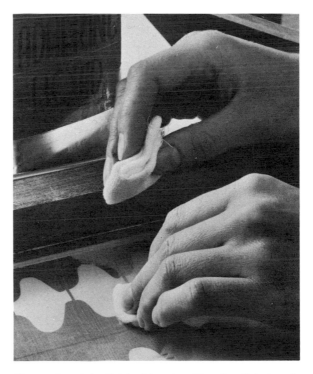

The quality of the finished handcut film stencil is largely determined by the care exercised in adhering it to the screen. Photo, courtesy The American Crayon Co., New Jersey.

brand new screens as well as to those that have been reclaimed. Even if the screen mesh appears to be clean, further steps are necessary to prepare it for receiving the film stencil.

Newly stretched screens must be given a brisk wash to remove any sizing, which though invisible to the eye could impede proper adhesion. Use hot water and a household cleanser like Ajax or a similar product; brush both sides of the screen simultaneously with a pair of nail brushes. Follow with a cold water rinse to flush away any vestige of the cleanser. Allow the screen to dry naturally. Reclaimed screens must be given the same treatment to remove any residual grease, ink, or solvent.

To establish perfect contact between film and screen fabric—a necessary condition for good adhering—it's helpful to place several sheets of cardboard underneath the art bearing the film, during the adhering procedure.

Use only the adhering fluid recommended by the manufacturer of the film. Film and fluid must be compatible for best adhering results.

Make certain that the wiping cloths used for adhering are clean and absorbent. Flannel or cotton is fine; nylon and other nonabsorbent synthetics won't do the job as well.

Keep an electric fan blowing on the screen during the adhesion of the film. A flow of air will help to evaporate the adhering fluid quickly, before it has a chance to dissolve the film.

It's important to allow the film to dry thoroughly before stripping the backing sheet. Premature stripping may lift up film edges or pull along some of the elements of the design image, impairing the quality of the stencil.

If, for whatever reason, re-adhering should prove necessary (in part or totally), the backing sheet must be replaced. Adhering fluid applied to the film without the backing sheet will spread, and in so doing, will invariably dissolve the film and ruin the stencil.

After the adhering is complete and the backing sheet peeled off, it's a good idea to wipe the underside of the screen with a cloth dampened with mineral spirits. Wiping in this manner clears the screen mesh of any trace of adhesive (used in the manufacture of the film).

Achieving Textural Effects

Although the film stencil technique is at its best for lettering, poster-type illustration, and hard-edge graphic design, some textural effects are possible.

The line cutter, previously mentioned, can, if artfully handled, create interesting crosshatching and stippling textures. For dot-etch effects, a small soldering iron with interchangeable tips—the kind used by hobbycrafters—can be adapted for work on lacquer film with moderate success. Each momentary touch of the heated tip melts the film at the point of contact, producing an open dot. With the dots burned in, and main elements of the stencil cut, the film is adhered to the screen in the conventional manner. A soft-edge effect can, within limitations, be introduced by partially dissolving film edges with a brush, sponge, or wiping cloth moistened with adhering fluid. This can be done either before or after the stencil is adhered.

Reclaiming the Screen

To remove lacquer film from the screen, wet the underside with a lacquer solvent commercially known as "film remover." (This is similar to, but more chemically potent than, adhering fluid.) Then, lay the screen down over a spread of several sheets of large newspapers. Pour a generous quantity of the solvent into the screen and swish it around with a soft rag. You'll note that after a few minutes the stencil image begins to dissolve and disintegrate. When you lift the screen and pull away the newspaper, most of the film will come off with it.

Any film remaining on the screen can be removed by briskly rubbing both sides with rags saturated with the solvent. As this type of solvent is quite volatile, it's important that you wipe it off immediately before it has a chance to dry into the screen. Solvent that has so dried will form a cloudy haze and block the open mesh.

Reclaiming a screen made with water-soluble film is comparatively simple. All you do to dissolve the stencil is to place the screen in a sink, and hose it down with a strong spray of hot water.

(Left) Red Reflection *by Richard Anuszkiewicz, courtesy Steve Poleskie, New York. This hard-edge linear composition lends itself amiably to the handcut film technique.*

Jackie Kennedy Montage *by Andy Warhol, courtesy Harry N. Abrams, Inc. New York.*
This high contrast print montage was produced with a photostencil.

CHAPTER EIGHT

Photographic stencil methods

Modern photostencil technology is based on a photochemical principle discovered way back in 1852, long before screen printing, as we know it today, existed. The discovery is associated with the work of William H. Fox Talbot. In experimenting with photographic processes for etching on steel, Talbot found that when he added a photosensitive salt, such as potassium bichromate, to a gelatin emulsion and exposed it to light, the emulsion hardened, and became insoluble in water. He concluded that light energy has an actinic effect on a sensitized colloid, changing it chemically from a soluble state to an insoluble state.

The extension of this principle to photostencil preparation may be hypothetically demonstrated in the following manner.

Let's assume that we coat the surface of the screen with a sensitized gelatin emulsion, and allow it to dry. We then place an opaque object—say, a coin—on the emulsion coating and expose the emulsion to a source of light. When we remove the coin and wash the screen with water, here's what we'd find. The water has washed away only that part of the emulsion that was shielded from the light, that is, the part covered by the coin; the rest of the emulsion, the part *exposed* to the light, has *not* washed away. The result is a "stencil" consisting of a small, round area in open mesh, surrounded by a hardened coating of emulsion.

In actual practice, of course, the stencil image isn't limited to the use of a physical object as a device for obstructing the passage of light, although experimentally interesting effects can be achieved in that manner. In routine procedures for making photostencils, the design to be printed is reproduced by handmade or camera-made transparencies on which the design image is delineated in opaque form.

The application of photography to stencil preparation has extended the scope of screen printing enormously both as a creative art medium and as a commercial reproduction process. With photographically produced stencils, it's possible to print the finest detail with unerring fidelity to the original work, be it pictorial composition, lettering, or type matter. Within the technical range of possibilites are facsimile reproductions of photographs, transfer letter-ing, benday dots, and a host of other mechanical tints and textures.

Where intricacy of detail is an important element in the design, photographic stencils often can be prepared in a shorter time than it would normally take to do the job with other stencil making methods. Often as not, the photostencil method is the only practical one by which a design can be reproduced. Photographic stencils are very durable and can withstand editions running into the thousands.

In this chapter we'll take up the two basic methods of preparing stencils photographically: the *direct* method (the one employed in our hypothetical demonstration), and the *transfer* method. In the direct method the screen fabric is coated with a liquid emulsion that has been made light sensitive; the *transfer* or indirect method involves the use of a sensitized film tissue that's transferred and adhered to the screen.

There's no unanimity of professional opinion as to which of the two is the "better" method. Preference for one or the other depends in large measure on specific production requirements. It's good to gain experience in both.

What You'll Need to Prepare Photostencils

To gain initial experience with both the direct and transfer methods of photostencil preparation, you'll need the following basic materials.

Equipment and supplies: A camera isn't an indispensable requisite, nor is a darkroom. But you'll need to keep certain supplies on hand such as photofilm, emulsion, and sensitizer (all are available from your regular screen supply dealer). You'll also need a tray or two, rubber gloves or tongs, spray hose, water thermometer, measuring cup, timer, and a low wattage safelight bulb.

You may include in your purchasable equipment a professional contact frame for exposures. But with a sheet of plate glass, and felt or rubber padding mounted to a backboard, you can easily improvise an exposure contact arrangement yourself. This will serve the purpose adequately, and is adaptable for both the direct and transfer methods.

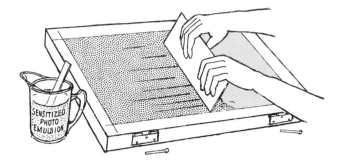

Coating the screen with sensitized photo emulsion.

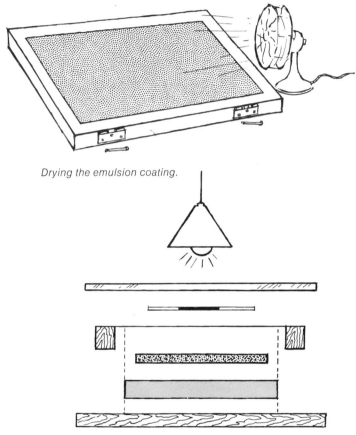

Drying the emulsion coating.

Schematic view of a simple contact setup for an overhead exposure.

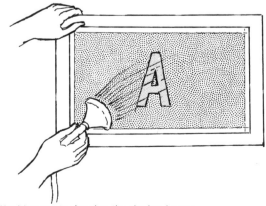

Washing out to develop the design image.

As for exposure lights, the most effective source of light for photographic exposures is free; that's the sun. Sunlight contains the greatest concentration of ultraviolet rays. It's these rays which act upon the sensitized emulsion. However, sunlight can't be relied upon or controlled, fluctuating as it does with time of day, weather, and season; therefore, it's necessary to equip yourself with an artificial light source. As a start, a good source of light is a #2 photoflood reflector bulb.

Photostencil positives: In both methods, a *positive* (an opaque image of the design on a transparent surface) is an essential element in producing a photostencil. Positives are prepared either by *hand* or by *camera*.

If the positive is prepared by hand, the design image is painted, drawn, or otherwise applied with an opaquing medium onto a sheet of clear acetate or other transparent material. The design image may be traced from accurately prepared black-and-white art or rendered freely with only a rough sketch to go by. Either way, the final image on a handsome positive must be confined to a "line" technique. In the lexicon of the graphic arts the term "line" technique includes solids, lines, stipple, crosshatching, dry-brush, and spatter.

There's no such restriction of technique when the positive is prepared by camera, because the camera can be made to pick up graded tones or halftones as well as line work. What's more, the camera can reduce, enlarge, or keep the design image the same size. Well over 90% of all positives for photostencil work are prepared by camera. However, it takes special cameras and related facilities to produce professionally acceptable positives. Most screen printers, therefore, find it more expedient to order their positives from photoservices rather than prepare these positives themselves. No matter how the positive is produced—whether by hand or by camera—it serves the same function in the photographic procedure of stencil making.

The Direct Method

In the direct method, the procedure calls for coating the screen with a liquid photographic emulsion which ultimately becomes the stencil tissue. Photographic emulsion is available in two forms: one comes presensitized; the other must be sensitized by the user. The latter is, by far, the more popular because it can be prepared as needed, thus assuring maximum freshness. It also makes much shorter exposures possible.

With the exception of the step which deals with sensitizing the emulsion, the general procedure outlined below applies to both types of emulsion.

Step 1. Check the screen fabric: It must be completely free of sizing, grease, dust, or other impurities. Wash and rub down both sides of the screen with hot water and a sprinkling of cleansing powder.

Then rinse thoroughly, making sure to remove all traces of the cleanser. Give the screen a final cold water rinse, and allow it to dry naturally.

Step 2. Sensitize the emulsion: This step entails making up a bichromate sensitizing solution, and adding it to the emulsion. Follow the instructions given in the manufacturer's data sheet.

For example, the directions may require you to dissolve 2 oz. of ammonium bichromate in one pint of lukewarm water. This sensitizing solution is then added to the emulsion in the ratio of 1:5, that is, one part sensitizing solution to five parts emulsion.

You needn't be overly concerned about observing strict darkroom precautions when preparing sensitized emulsion. In its wet state, sensitized emulsion is *not* affected by light; it becomes light sensitive only upon drying. The general practice is to work under *subdued* illumination.

Step 3. Apply the sensitized emulsion to the screen: Place the screen (fabric side up) on a flat work table or straddle it across two saw horses. Pour some sensitized emulsion—enough to cover the entire screen area—into one end of the screen. With a sharp-edged piece of rigid cardboard or commercial applicator, squeegee the emulsion across the screen. Make sure to get even and complete coverage.

Allow the sensitized emulsion to dry and then apply a second coat in the same manner. With the use of a fan, the first coat will dry in less than twenty minutes; the second coat will take ten minutes or so. The first coat seals the mesh; the second builds up the required deposit of emulsion. Drying should take place in a dark, dust-free area.

Step 4. Set up for the exposure: The procedure outlined here is based on use of the simple contact arrangement previously mentioned—namely, the padded backboard and sheet of glass.

Position the sensitized screen (with the fabric side facing up) over the padded backboard. Using several blocks of wood, books, or layers of cardboard, build up the backboard so that the padding and screen fabric are in close contact. Understandably, the padded backboard, which serves as a contact platform, must be somewhat smaller than the inside of the screen frame.

Center the positive (image side facing down) on the screen, and place the sheet of glass on top of it. A weight at each end of the glass will help keep it pressed firmly against the positive, and assure perfect contact.

The contact setup as it's now arranged is meant for overhead exposure. The light rays pass through in the following order: first, the glass; then, the back side of the positive; and last, the sensitized surface of the screen.

Step 5. Expose the screen: Rig up the #2 photoflood reflector bulb so that it's about 18″ or 20″ above

the contact setup. Set the interval timer and switch on the light for a five-minute exposure.

The exposure time mentioned here is merely an approximation. Length of exposure varies with the distance and the nature of the light source. But there are other variables such as the intensity of the light, the nature of the positive, the type and freshness of the emulsion, the area of the sensitized surface—even the humidity in the air. Since these conditions are so changeable, it's good practice to run several exposure tests beforehand.

Step 6. Wash out the screen: With the screen held upright in a large sink or drain tub, direct a fairly strong spray of warm water to both sides. As the unexposed areas of the emulsion wash away, you'll see the stencil image on the screen begin to appear and take shape. Continue washing until the image is sharp and clear. This should take no more than a few minutes and can be done under normal illumination.

For best results, wash the screen as soon after exposure as practical. If a delay is unavoidable, store the screen in a cool, dark area.

Step 7. Dry the screen: Place the screen between several sheets of blotting paper (white newsprint will do). Press down firmly to absorb excess water. Then allow the screen to dry naturally or by fan.

Step 8. Check the screen: Following the usual procedure, check the stencil to be sure that it's free of pinholes or leaks. Touch up where necessary. When the screen is hooked up on the printing bed, and register guides set in place, the stencil is ready for ink and squeegee.

A photostencil made with the direct method has remarkable durability, because the emulsion which carries the stencil image is embedded in the screen mesh. Properly prepared, a direct photostencil will last for thousands of sharp impressions. It's adaptable for printing with any type of ink formulation—water based, oil based, lacquer, synthetic, etc.

The Transfer Method

There's a basic difference between the direct method, just described, and the transfer method. In the direct method the photo emulsion is applied directly to the screen in fluid form. Upon drying it's exposed and developed to create the stencil image. In the transfer method, the photo emulsion, in the form of a specially prepared film, is exposed and developed *first*. Later it's *transferred* to the screen as a stencil tissue.

The photofilm used in the transfer method consists of a sheet of gelatin or emulsion supported on a clear polyester backing. It comes in two forms—*presensitized* and *unsensitized*. Of the two, the presensitized is gaining in popularity, especially for studio and classroom use. This presensitized photofilm is employed in the procedure outlined below. Assuming that you use the same simple contact and

Harriet Hubbard Ayer Poster, *25" x 38", edition—750, courtesy Paint Print Process Co., New York. Fourteen separate stencils were used to reproduce this multicolor poster; some were photographic, others tusche-glue resist.*

exposure setup as in the direct method, here are the necessary steps.

Step 1. Check the screen fabric: The screen fabric must be immaculately clean to ensure good results. This is particularly true when the screen is to be used with photofilm. Follow the cleaning procedure suggested for the direct method.

Step 2. Cut the photofilm to size: Photofilm is packaged in rolls or sheets. Cut a section an inch or two larger than the design image on the positive, replacing the rest in its original wrapper. Unlike camera-speed films, this type of photofilm isn't instantly responsive to light. It can be normally handled under subdued illumination, away from sunlight or bright fluorescent lights. A safelight bulb is best.

Step 3. Set up for the exposure: Place the film, emulsion side down, on the padded backboard. (The emulsion side is the one which appears tacky when touched with a moist finger.) Center the positive, image side facing down, over the film. Cover with the sheet of glass, placing weights at each end to ensure good contact between positive and film.

Step 4. Expose the screen: The same factors which affect exposure time in the direct method—type of light, intensity, distance away from the sensitized surface, etc.—also apply to photofilm exposures as well. Generally speaking, exposure time is longer for presensitized photofilms and emulsions, than for those which are sensitized by the user prior to exposure. As with the direct method, the right exposure time is best determined through tests.

Step 5. Develop the film: Presensitized film must go through a developing process before the stencil image can be washed out. The developing process produces a chemical change in the emulsion, making it insoluble in water. In the technical language of the photochemist, the developing solution (an oxidizing agent) releases energy which causes the molecules of the light-exposed emulsion to link up. Thus the emulsion changes from a soluble to an insoluble state.

Manufacturers of photofilms supply the two basic chemicals needed for making up the developing solution. These come conveniently measured out in separate packets, with specific directions for mixing. The procedure is simple and can be carried out in subdued light.

To develop the film, here's what you do. Immediately or soon after exposure, immerse the film, emulsion side up, in a tray containing the developing solution. Rock the tray gently to stimulate the action of the developing solution. After a minute or so remove the film, and place it, emulsion side up, on a sheet of glass or other hard, nonabsorbent surface. At this stage the film is ready for the next step, which is washing out.

Note that because developing solution generates

a strong gas, it should *not* be stored in a stoppered bottle. The safest thing to do is to discard whatever solution is not used the same day.

Step 6. Wash out the film: Direct a gentle stream of warm water (about 95°F.) onto the surface of the film. Within a minute or two, you'll see the design image emerge and take shape as the part of the emulsion, shielded by the positive during the exposure, dissolves and washes away. Continue washing for a minute after the design image has become clearly visible. Finish off with a spray of cold water to chill the film. Now the film is ready to be transferred to the screen.

Step 7. Adhere the film: Right after washing out the film, place it (still supported on the sheet of glass) in position on the printing bed. That done, carefully lower the screen on its hinges and press down firmly. Make sure that perfect contact is established between fabric and film. Place a sheet of newsprint or paper toweling on the screen, and with the palm of the hand rub lightly across it to absorb the excess water. Continue this blotting action, changing papers when necessary, until all moisture is gone. Allow the film to dry. Use a fan if you want to hasten the drying.

Step 8: Remove the backing sheet: When the film is thoroughly dry, raise the screen. You'll note that the entire film tissue has fully adhered to the underside of the screen fabric. The backing sheet must now be removed to open the stencil. To do this, lift the sheet at one corner and gently pull it away from the film. When the adhering is right, the backing sheet will come off easily.

Step 9. Mask out the screen area surrounding the stencil tissue: Since the film area is usually made smaller than the screen, the open mesh surrounding the film must be masked out. Use lacquer, glue, paper, or any other suitable mask-out medium.

Step 10. Check the stencil: Inspect the stencil for pinholes and leaks, and touch up where necessary with an appropriate mask-out medium. When that's done, the stencil is ready for printing.

The transfer method of photostencil preparation is unexcelled in its faithful and sharp reproduction of detail. With normal care, a photostencil made with the transfer method (though not as durable as one made with the direct method) will hold up well for extended editions before showing signs of wear.

Checkpoints in Photostencil Preparation

When preparing your photostencils, it's helpful to prepare a checklist such as the following one. In this way you can guard against forgetting any of the necessary steps or checkpoints.

The positive
(1) Is the design image opaque?

Cutting a strip of photofilm to required size.

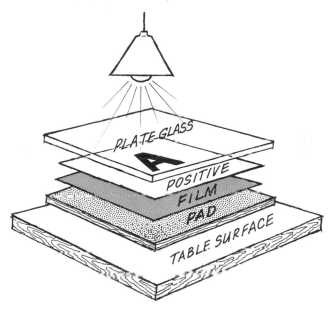

Schematic view of a simple contact setup for an overhead exposure.

Developing the film.

Washing out the design image.

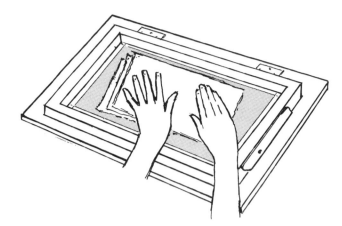

Adhering the photofilm to the screen.

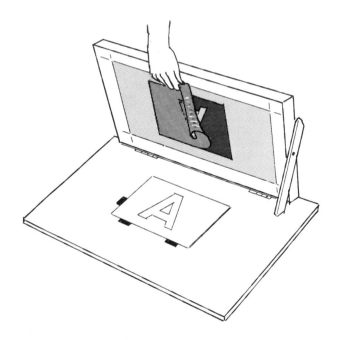

Peeling off the backing sheet to open up the stencil.

Blocking out the open screen area surrounding the stencil.

(2) Are the transparent areas of the positive spotless? You can't make a good stencil with a faulty positive.

The contact setup

(3) Is the glass free of smudges and specks? These may show up as imperfections in the stencil.

(4) Is there perfect contact between positive and sensitized surface? The sharpness of the stencil image depends upon it.

The exposure

(5) Did you make preliminary tests to establish correct exposure time? There are too many variables to assume that exposure time will always be the same.

Developing and washing out

(6) Are chemical components mixed correctly?

(7) Is the water the right temperature? Specifications vary with different products. Be sure to follow the data sheet issued by the manufacturer.

The screen fabric

(8) Has the fabric been properly treated to accept the stencil tissue? Unless the fabric is free from sizing, grease, or other impurities, the bond between emulsion and fabric will be weak, and a poor stencil will result.

About Equipment

The procedures for preparing screens photographically, described before, were based on using equipment you may assemble at nominal cost or may already have on hand. A good course to follow is to gain experience with the simplest components, and add to your stock of tools and professional equipment as the occasion warrants.

Professional contact setups: There are two types of setups: contact-print frames and vacuum contact units.

☐ *Contact-print frames*—These come in different sizes and in various types. In all of them, a glass plate and padded backboard are coordinated as a portable unit. The glass is set into a rigid, nonwarp frame made to fit over the padded backboard; the two components are held together by a metal clamp or spring device.

☐ *Vacuum contact units*—The vacuum suction principle is the distinguishing operational feature of all vacuum contact units. The suction action of a vacuum pump draws the sensitized surface and the positive firmly together in an airtight enclosure creating the ideal contact condition for exposures.

Vacuum contact units come in different types. Some have built-in light systems; some do not. Some are portable; others are heavily constructed floor units intended as permanent installations. Among the leading manufacturers of vacuum contact units and related equipment is the nuArc Company, best known for its Flip-top models which are extensively used throughout the graphic arts industry.

Exposure lights: Photoflood bulbs, sun lamps, blacklight fluorescent lamps, and carbon arc lamps can be used for exposures.

□ *Photoflood bulbs*—#2 photoflood reflector bulbs may be used singly or in multiples, depending upon the area to be exposed. They have a lightlife of five to six hours, but because they lose intensity with continued use, the exposure time must be compensated for proportionately.

□ *Sun lamps*—Rich in ultraviolet rays, sun lamps make a good light source for photographic stencil exposures. Like photoflood bulbs, they fit into standard light sockets.

□ *Blacklight fluorescent lamps*—These lamps are available in tubes of varying lengths, the same as ordinary fluorescent lights. The blacklight fluorescent lamp has a special interior coating within the tube that emits light with a high concentration of ultraviolet rays. The chief advantage of this type of fluorescent light is its ability to generate a minimum amount of heat. Therefore, this light can be brought closer to the surface being exposed than any other light source.

□ *Carbon arc lamps*—A carbon arc lamp doesn't use filament bulbs or gaseous tubes. It operates on an entirely different principle. It employs a set of carbon rods (resembling sticks of hardened charcoal) which serve as electrodes. The rods face each other, head on, but don't actually touch. When the current is turned on, it arcs across the rods. The tips heat up, forming a vaporous gas which ignites, producing an intensely brilliant and steady light.

About Handmade Positives

Presented below are some notes on tracing surfaces, opaquing media, and special effects.

Tracing surfaces: Here are four different types of surfaces on which a design may be traced and a positive produced.

□ *Patented tracing tissues*—Sold under such trade names as Trace-o-lene, Trace-O-Mat, and Dul-Mat, these tissues provide excellent surfaces for opaquing handmade positives. They come in clear or frosted finishes, as well as in a number of different weights.

□ *Tracing paper*—Ordinary tracing paper with good see-through visibility can be used for making positives. Tracing paper is put up in rolls and sheets, but sheets will prove to be better for the purpose, as paper cut from a roll has a tendency to curl.

□ *Bond paper*—Any good quality bond paper is serviceable for positives. It should be flat, and free from wrinkles. If the paper lacks sufficient transparency,

mineral spirits or oil rubbed over the back will help considerably.

□ *Glass*—While glass offers maximum transparency, its highly polished, somewhat slippery surface makes it difficult to draw or paint on. Thus, the range of art techniques and opaquing media that can be used is limited. Glass has one compensatory feature: it can be used repeatedly for different designs since the opaque image washes off with the proper solvents.

Opaquing media: Included in this category are such items as inks and paints, liquid frisket, photoengraver's opaquing compound, and crayons as well as handcut masking film.

□ *Inks and paints*—India ink and tempera paint (preferably black) are good media for opaquing in the design image. For nonabsorbent surfaces, such as acetate or glass, quick drying oil based paints work well when reduced to a brushing consistency. Avoid diluting the opaquing medium (whatever it may be) to the point of a wash tone. To be effective, the design image painted on a positive must be opaque and lightproof.

□ *Liquid frisket latex*—This is a water based, latex composition possessing excellent opacity. Thinned to a proper brushing consistency, it adheres well to any surface, yet is easy to remove.

□ *Photoengravers' opaquing compound*—Commercially, this is the most widely used of the opaquing media. It applies easily with brush, ruling pen, or other art tools. Usually deep brown in color, it's lightproof, covers in one coat, adheres to all surfaces, and dries quickly.

□ *Crayons*—Any type of wax crayon in pencil or stick form may be used for making positives if it will produce an opaque image. There's no restriction on color, but black and deep red possess superior opacity over the others. Litho pencils, China pencils, and Conté crayons work best, because they're exceptionally opaque, don't rub off, and are easy to apply on both absorbent and nonabsorbent surfaces.

□ *Handcut masking films*—Masking film used for preparing handmade positives is a red or an amber-colored film tissue. Though optically transparent, it's photographically lightproof. Like regular stencil film, it too is laminated to a plastic backing sheet and is cut with a stencil knife. In preparing the positive, the design is tracecut just deep enough to incise the film layer without cutting into the backing sheet. The area surrounding the design is stripped away, leaving the design delineated in film. When the positive is exposed, the design in film will block out the light; the stripped away area, now in clear plastic, will allow the light to go through.

Masking films are sold under such trade names as Rubylith and Amberlith (there are others). They're especially effective where mechanical, knife-cut

Here's a sampling of the great variety of tonal and textural effects achievable with mechanical shading sheets combined with photostencils.

sharpness is an essential requirement in the photo-stencil. Masking films offer other decided working advantages. Large design areas take very little more time than small areas because there's no filling in to do. A negative image (if desired) is as easy to achieve as a positive one; it's merely a matter of which part of the film is selected for stripping. Then too, since the film is uniformly lightproof, there are no pinholes or leaks to touch up, as is often the case when working with conventional opaquing media.

Special effects: Here are three methods of achieving special effects.

☐ *Texture sheets*—These sheets can mechanically produce dotted, linear, or other textural effects with a uniformity that's difficult, if not impossible, to achieve by hand. Most art supply stores stock a variety of them.

Texture sheets come in dozens of different patterns preprinted in opaque inks on transparent tissue. When applied to a positive, the selected pattern becomes an integral part of the design image. Similar sheets are available in many lettering styles and standard typefaces, all of which can be transferred or otherwise applied to the positive and incorporated into the design.

☐ *Photograms*—It's possible to create realistic silhouette effects or "photograms" as they're called, by placing an actual object directly on the sensitized surface or the glass plate covering it. This procedure, in effect, achieves the same objective as a conventional positive. The choice of objects that lend themselves to photograms is infinite: keys, hairpins, coins, rings, chickenwire, matchsticks, etc. In addition to such three-dimensional objects, you can experiment with leaves, construction paper, aluminum foil, masking tape, or any other lightproof material. All this material can be used in its natural form or shaped by cutting, tearing, or perforating. You may also want to use a sprinkling of flock, black pepper, sand, and other granular substances to produce novel textures and surface configurations.

☐ *Drypoint techniques*—Though limited in its commercial applications, a positive made in the manner of a drypoint etching plate offers interesting possibilities for the creative screen printer.

Briefly here's the procedure. Place a sheet of heavy-gauge celluloid or similar hard surfaced plastic over a prepared line drawing. With an engraver's needle or other sharp pointed tool, trace-scratch the lines of the drawing on the celluloid surface. Rub an opaque ink into the engraved lines. Remove whatever ink is left on the surface with a cloth dampened with solvent; then wipe dry. The opaque line image on the celluloid comprises the positive.

About Camera-Made Positives

To make positives photographically, whether for line or halftone reproduction, the original art is exposed in front of a special camera, called a *process camera*. The image is picked up by the lens, and when developed, a film negative results in which the relationship between the black and white areas on the art is reversed. What's black on the art is white (transparent) on the negative and vice versa. Subsequently, through an additional step, the negative is converted to a positive which re-establishes the true black-and-white relationship of the art.

With halftone positives any painting, drawing, or photograph can be reproduced by converting continuous tones into individual dots. To prepare this type of positive, a half-tone screen is interposed between the lens and the film within the camera. This halftone screen consists of a gridwork of finely ruled lines etched on a glass plate. This screen breaks up the total image into dots of varying size. Darker tones are represented by larger dots in close proximity to each other; lighter tones are represented by smaller dots, relatively widely spaced. The tonal range is from practically 100% black to almost pure white—at least it appears so when viewed without the aid of a magnifying glass.

Halftone positives are identified by "line" number, most often from 45 to 133. A 45-line halftone, for example, has 45 ruled lines per linear inch; this results in 2,025 (45 x 45) apertures or individual dots per square inch. A 65-line halftone will have 4,225 (65 x 65) dots per square inch. The higher the line number, the smaller and less conspicuous the dots. While it's visually desirable to reduce the relative

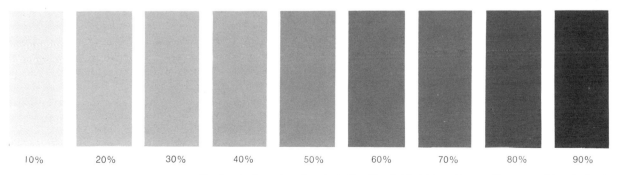

| 10% | 20% | 30% | 40% | 50% | 60% | 70% | 80% | 90% |

Mechanical overlays for photostencil reproduction make a wide range of tonal effects achievable with one printing. Above is a sample of a tonal scale of values with specific percentage identification.

This screen print was reproduced from an old engraving using the photostencil method. Courtesy the Ulano Products Co., Inc., New York.

size of the dots to the smallest size possible, there are technical difficulties encountered all along the way—in producing the positive, making the photo-stencil, and printing from it. For practical reasons, therefore, it's safest to stay within the 45- to 65-line range.

Ordering positives from a photoservice: When ordering, remember to ink in four small crossmarks (one at each corner) within the margin area of the art. These will physically assist in positioning the stencil when setting the register guides.

Indicate the desired *size* of the positive. If it's to be the same size as the art, the usual notation is *s.s.* If it's to be enlarged or reduced, show in either case, only one of the dimensions. Modifications in size are photographically proportionate.

Designate halftones by *line number,* for example, "45-line", "65-line", etc.

Specify that you want the design image to be applied to the *underside* of the transparency. That way, the lettering or pictorial image will appear facing the right way when viewed from the top surface.

Check the art carefully. Smudges or fingerprints will show up in the positive; retouching costs are expensive.

About Formulas and Procedures for Sensitizing Photofilms

Formulas for making up the sensitizing solution vary with different films. Therefore, follow the photofilm manufacturer's recommendations. The basic ingredient in most sensitizing solutions is a bichromate salt, which may either be a potassium, sodium, or an ammonium bichromate.

Sensitizing solution can be applied to the film by means of dipping, rolling on, or brushing, but many manufacturers of photofilms recommend the brushing method. Whichever method you use, it's important that the entire emulsion surface of the film receive a smooth, even coating of sensitizing solution.

Sensitizing should take place in subdued light, preferably in a curtained-off area illuminated by a safelight bulb. When the film is dry, it's exposed and washed out in the same way as presensitized film, except that the developing phase is unnecessary.

In its mixed state, a bichromate sensitizing solution should be kept in a lightproof, brown bottle. Stored in a dark, cool place, it has a shelflife of several weeks.

A word of caution: bichromates are poisonous and can cause serious skin irritation to those subject to dermatological allergies. It's good shop practice to use rubber gloves when handling bichromate solutions.

About Photostencil Exposures

Bear in mind that heat has a damaging effect on photo emulsions. When using photoflood bulbs, sun lamps, or other heat generating light sources, it's a good plan to keep an electric fan going to drive off the heat, especially during extended exposures.

Use strong lights at maximum capacity. A short exposure with a strong light will give better results than a prolonged exposure with a weak light. From time to time, it's good to check the light source to be sure it hasn't seriously diminished in intensity. This is particularly important with photoflood bulbs which gradually and imperceptibly lose intensity.

When increasing the distance of the light source to provide greater coverage of the sensitized surface, an acquaintance with a well known law of physics, pertaining to light, will come in handy in determining the relative change in exposure time. The Law of Inverse Squares states that the amount of light of a point source falling on an object is inversely proportional to the square of the distance from the source of the object. In practice, this means that if you double the distance between the light and the sensitized surface, the exposure time will be four times as long. Conversely, if you reduce the distance by one-half, exposure time will be cut to one-fourth.

For a stencil where extra durability is desired, expose relatively longer. Bear in mind, however, that you risk loss of fine detail with overexposure.

When sensitizing with a bichromate solution, the design image will wash out best if you allow a minimum amount of time to elapse between sensitizing and exposing.

A trial test prior to full-scale exposure eliminates guesswork in that it takes into account not only the intensity of light, but all other factors contributing to the outcome of the exposure.

About Positioning the Photofilm Stencil on the Screen

To determine the exact position of the design image on the screen in relation to the stock to be printed, the following suggestion will prove helpful.

Position and tape the positive onto a cardboard of the same size as the stock you'll be printing on. Lower the screen on its hinges, and center the design image as you see it through the screen. Then, raise the screen, and fasten the register guides to fit the cardboard. When the film is ready to be adhered, place it (emulsion side up) on the positive which is still attached to the cardboard, so that the crossmarks of film and positive match up. Then, lower the screen, and adhere in the usual manner. The cardboard on which the positive is mounted also serves as a pack-up, assuring good contact between film and screen fabric.

About Screen Fabrics

In commercial practice, nylon, dacron, and other synthetic fabrics are widely used for photostencils. The beginner, however, will find it easier to work with silk, which offers a more receptive bonding surface for the film tissue.

For all routine work, #12 silk (or its mesh equivalent in other fabrics) is adequate. For exceedingly fine detail or halftones over 60-line, a #14 or #16 mesh is recommended, not only because the stencil will yield sharper prints, but it will probably hold up longer as well.

Regardless of choice of fabric or size of mesh, it can't be emphasized too strongly that the screen fabric *must* be scrupulously clean. Any trace of sizing, grease, dirt, or other impurities will impede proper adhesion.

About Reclaiming Photoscreens

Stencils made by the transfer photofilm method are considerably easier to reclaim than those made with the direct emulsion method. In a film-type photoscreen, the stencil tissue clings to the surface of the mesh; in an emulsion-type screen, the stencil tissue is virtually embedded in the mesh.

To remove a *film-type* photostencil, sponge both sides of the screen with hot water. Let the screen soak for a while until the stencil tissue shows signs of softening. Rub down briskly with a small nailbrush, concentrating mostly on the film side; then hose down with a forceful spray of hot water. Nearly all of the film will, by this time, have come off. Any film particles stubbornly clinging to the mesh will respond to a wash with an enzyme. Whenever an enzyme is used in reclaiming a screen, it must be neutralized, or the next stencil will be weakened or seriously impaired. To neutralize the enzyme, wash the screen with a diluted vinegar solution (one part vinegar, one part water). Follow up with a cold water rinse and allow the screen to dry.

To remove an *emulsion-type* photostencil, follow the same procedure. However, it will take greater effort to dislodge the emulsion from the screen mesh, especially if this is done long after the printing has been completed. When a direct emulsion photoscreen is stored for a length of time it becomes difficult—sometimes impossible—to reclaim the screen.

About Different Types of Photofilms

Photofilms are sold under various manufacturer's trade names. Each manufacturer offers an assortment of presensitized and unsensitized films to meet specific requirements in terms of fidelity of reproduction, durability, affinity for selected screen fabrics, etc. Regardless of brand name or special purpose, the basic operational procedures outlined in this chapter apply to most films. Some, however, to a greater or lesser extent, depart from routine procedures. Typical of these are the Ulano Wetshot Photofilm, carbon tissue, and duPont Screen Process Film.

Ulano Wetshot Photofilm: This film, which is sensitized by the user, is popular with many busy craftsmen. It lends itself to fast production, possesses excellent dimensional stability, and produces sharp,

durable stencils. Its identifying feature is that it can be exposed immediately after sensitizing without waiting for the sensitizer to dry.

The film is sensitized with a bichromate sensitizer. A sheet of kraft paper (brown wrapping paper) cut to the same size as the film is soaked with the sensitizer and placed on top of the wet film. Kraft paper and film (now sandwiched together) are blotted, wiped dry, and then exposed through the back of the film. The exposed film, kraft paper side up, is immersed in a tray full of warm water. Within fifteen or twenty seconds the kraft paper loosens up sufficiently to be peeled off. The washing out is then continued until the design image emerges, sharp and clear. The wet film, emulsion side up, is transferred to the screen and adhered in the usual manner.

Carbon tissue: Sometimes called *pigment paper* or *autotype tissue,* carbon tissue comes in both presensitized and unsensitized form. It has special procedures for exposing it in the wet or dry state. In the main, the method involves transferring a patented paper-backed gelatin tissue onto a temporary polyester support, and subsequently re-transferring the gelatin tissue to the screen. This may be classified as a double-transfer photostencil method.

Historically, the carbon tissue method is one of the earliest and, to many oldtimers in the screen printing industry, still one of the favorite methods of photostencil preparation. Carbon tissue originated in England some 100 years ago. It was first used to etch photographic printing rollers in the textile and wallpaper industries. Introduced in the United States in the late twenties, the carbon tissue method has, until recent developments of simpler methods, remained unchallenged in photostencil techniques.

duPont Screen Process Film: This is a presensitized camera-speed photographic film supported on a vinyl base. After processing, it's stripped from the base to become the actual screen printing stencil. The duPont film is unique in that it can be exposed by projection in a camera, or in the conventional way by direct contact. Exposure time is short. Ten sec. at 6′ with a 60-watt bulb for exposure by direct contact and 60 sec. for projection exposure are typical. With this film, darkroom and camera equipment are technical requirements. Since a camera is employed, it's possible to change the size of the design image in the process of making the stencil. However, the most important feature of the duPont Screen Process Film method is that the stencil image is produced directly from the art, without the use of a positive.

The duPont film (and others like it) may well be the forerunner of future developments in direct art-to-stencil preparation. In time, it may completely do away with the need for making a negative or a positive, thereby eliminating an intermediate step in photostencil techniques.

Detailed data sheets for the various types of photofilms are available from screen supply dealers.

CHAPTER NINE

Stencil preparation for multicolor printing

The various stencil making methods described in preceding chapters have been deliberately confined to reproducing a design in a single color. A basic understanding of the procedure for making stencils for single color reproduction is a technical prerequisite for multicolor work.

A design in two or more colors normally requires a separate stencil and a separate printing for each color. I say normally, because it's possible, as you'll see later, to print several colors at the same time, and to get a multiplicity of color effects through the technique of overprinting with transparent inks.

Multicolor Reproduction Using Opaque Inks

At this point let's discuss how to go about preparing stencils for multicolor reproduction when using *opaque* inks. Let's say we wish to reproduce a simple two color design which will require two stencils, one for each color. How to prepare each of these two stencils and get them to register in the print will be our present task. We'll assume that the design is centered on a white cardboard, the same size as the edition stock. The design to be reproduced consists of just two basic elements—a 5″ red circle, surrounded by a 1″ black border.

We'll use the handcut film stencil method and we'll print the job with oil based poster paints.

A number of preliminary steps are necessary, however, before proceeding with stencil preparation.

1. Draw crossmarks on the art: First, within the margin of the art, carefully pencil or ink in four small hairline crossmarks, one at each corner. These will serve as register marks for both cutting the stencil and printing the job.

2. Plan the color sequence: There aren't any hard and fast rules for determining the color sequence— which to print first, which second, and so on. But here are some general guidelines which will prove helpful.

When printing with inks that are *opaque,* it frequently works out best to print the background color or main element of the design first; the smaller elements later. Wherever feasible, light colors should be printed before dark ones. However, when em-

ploying *transparent* inks to achieve additional color effects, it's better to print darker colors ahead of the lighter ones. In lettering or in other design elements where outlines surround solid areas, it's advisable to print solid areas before outlines.

3. Make a notation of the sequence: Once you have decided upon the color sequence that's best for the job on hand, jot it down somewhere in the margin of the art, as a production note. In the present instance this would read:

Color #1 . . . Red
Color #2 . . . Black

The "production note" may not seem too important in a simple two color job such as this. However, in a more ambitious project involving many colors and many stencils, it will not only help you to keep track of the order in which the stencils should be made, but also maintain the sequence in which they're to be printed.

Preparing the Stencil for the First Color

The following steps illustrate the procedure for preparing and printing from the first color stencil.

Step 1. Cut the stencil: Tape a sheet of stencil film over the art, making sure the film is large enough to include the four crossmarks.

Tracecut the red area, extending it 1/16″ or so into the black. This extension, or "overdraw" as it's called, provides a margin of safety to compensate for slight discrepancies in register during printing. Now cut the lines of the crossmarks, making them as fine as possible.

Step 2. Strip the stencil: Strip the film within the cut areas. Don't forget to strip the crossmarks; for the time being, they're to be considered a part of the design.

Step 3. Adhere the stencil: Place the film (still attached to the art) on the printing bed. Center it under the screen, and set the guides in position. Take off most of the tape, leaving just enough to keep the film from shifting. Lower the screen and adhere the stencil in the usual manner. Then, peel away the backing sheet to open the design area. Remove the art from the bed. Block out the open screen surrounding the film, and set up for printing.

Step 4. Proceed with the printing operation: After pulling several *proofs* on the edition stock, check to see that everything is right. Then, block out the crossmarks with small strips of tape applied to the underside of the screen. When that's done, continue with the printing until the edition is complete.

Note: Save these *proof* sheets! You'll need them to check the register in the subsequent color.

Preparing the Stencil for the Second Color

The procedure for making the stencil for color #2 follows along the same lines as color #1, but with this important difference. This time, do *not* overdraw! The black, which is the second and finishing color, is cut to actual size. As before, tracecut the corresponding design area including the crossmarks. Strip the film, adhere it to the screen, peel the backing sheet, etc. The stencil for the second color is ready for ink and squeegee.

Before going ahead with the actual printing of the edition with color #2, pull impressions on the master proof sheets of the *first* color. Assuming that everything was done correctly, i.e., the stencils were cut and adhered accurately, the stock was placed snugly against the register guides, and there was no side to side movement of the screen, etc., then the crossmarks of the black (color #2) will coincide perfectly with those of the red (color #1). The alignment of the crossmarks indicates the alignment of both color areas of the design.

After blocking out the crossmarks and making the routine check for color match and printing quality, you can begin printing the edition. Because of the opaque character of the ink, the finished prints will not show any evidence of the overdraw.

When you print with opaque inks the procedure for getting stencils to register in multicolor work of three, five, ten, or any number of colors is essentially the same as for the two color job just described. Adjacent colors are overdrawn where necessary to assure proper alignment. This holds true no matter what stencil making technique you employ: handcut, blockout, resist, or photographic.

To print our hypothetical two color job with transparent inks, the stencil for the black as well as the stencil for the red would have to be cut with unvarying accuracy. That is, both colors must be exactly the size of the art, butting up against each other. Any extension of one color into another would show up as a distinct brown area where the two colors overlap.

When preparing a series of stencils, the overlapping and surprinting of transparent colors, if purposefully planned, can be a decided technical advantage; printing with transparent inks offers tremendous possibilities for obtaining a multiplicity of color effects. With three printings, for example, you can get seven colors; with four printings, fourteen colors; with five printings, twenty-eight. Theoretically, 896 color effects are possible with just ten printings.

The variegated, almost unlimited color effects achievable with transparent inks have a special appeal for artists who use screen printing as a creative art medium, rather than merely a duplicating process. In the commercial field, transparent inks are used mostly in the screening of textiles and wallpaper.

Considering the obvious economic advantage in stencil preparation and printings by using transparent inks, why work with opaque inks which, for the most part, require a separate stencil and a separate printing for each color? The prime reason is that by using opaque inks, it's possible to match the colors of the original art accurately and predictably. With transparent inks the colors in the art can only be approximated, because it's very difficult to determine the exact colors, shades, and tints which result from multiple overprintings. Transparent yellow printed over blue will unquestionably produce green, but not necessarily the particular shade of green to match the art. Transparent red over blue will produce a purple, but the purple which results from such overprinting will depend upon the particular red and particular blue selected, as well as the degree of transparency of the top color.

What's more, when printing with inks which aren't opaque, the order in which they're printed influences the results. For example, a green printed over red will result in a shade of brown not quite the same as that achieved by printing the red over green. Then too, stencils intended for printing with opaque inks are easier to prepare, since the color boundaries can be made to overlap one another without showing in the finished print.

Seasoned judgment, based on experience, will dictate when and which colors should be made opaque or transparent. The procedure for preparing the stencils and the order in which they're printed will depend upon that judgment.

Art for Multicolor Reproduction

All art designed for facsimile reproduction must be planned with clearly defined color areas. Each color area, no matter how small or incidental, must be separate and distinct. This technical requirement doesn't have equal relevance for the artist printer who uses the medium of screen printing to develop a graphic image extemporaneously, whether it be with opaque or transparent inks. Often he may not have a finished original piece of art to go by; instead, he develops the image stage by stage, color by color, as he proceeds with proofing and printing.

For the purpose of facsimile reproduction, whether as a fine art or a commercial printing process, distinct definition of color areas is a necessary factor in color separation for the preparation of stencils.

The component color areas on the art may be shown in their exact hues or merely outlined in the form of a key drawing with color notations indicated in pen or pencil. It's important, however, that the art, no matter how it's rendered, be the exact size of the edition stock. In this way the register guides can be set in the proper position.

Crossmarks

The finer they are, the better they'll serve the purpose for which they're intended. Instead of drawing in crossmarks by hand, you may want to use the kind of fine line crossmarks which come preprinted on rolls of transparent, self-adhesive tape. They're inexpensive; a roll of 200 costs less than a dollar.

If you plan to trim the stock after printing, the crossmarks can be positioned within the trim area; in which case, they can print throughout the run. This will provide a constant check on the accuracy of the register during the entire printing procedure.

Masking tape is effective for blocking out crossmarks when printing short runs. For extended editions, more durable mediums are lacquer, shellac, glue, or whatever is compatible with the nature of the stencil.

Register Adjustment

If, for whatever reason, the crossmarks of one color don't match up with those of the other colors in a multicolor job, a slight adjustment in the register guides on the printing bed is often all that is necessary to align them. This holds true if the crossmarks are consistently off in the same way. If they fluctuate from print to print (a rather serious problem!), the only remedy, at this time, is to use a flap guide device, the kind described in Chapter 14.

Preparing Stencils in Advance

The dimensional stability of cardboard and other printing stock is affected by changes in the weather. So too, to a greater or lesser extent, is stencil material such as glue, film, and photographic emulsion. It's unwise to prepare the entire series of stencils in a multicolor job before the actual printing. It's better to prepare one stencil at a time. Then, based on proofs of the preceding colors, corrections can be made in each stencil.

Transparent Color Charts

When preparing multicolor stencils for printing with transparent inks, it's important to preview the colors that can predictably be achieved through surprinting. The resulting color effects are so variable that ink manufacturers are reluctant to make transparent color charts available for distribution. Most printers

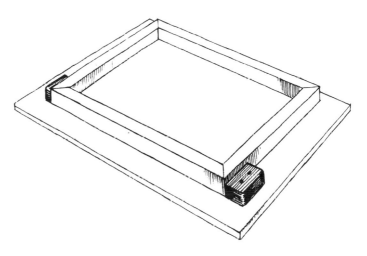

Two small blocks of wood fastened to the bed and snug against the screen frame prevent it from shifting side to side.

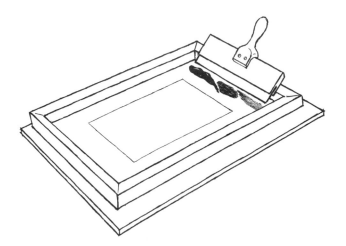

Blend preparation includes the mixing of distinct colors placed in desired positions within the screen.

Top: The first few impressions show distinct bands of color. Middle: Gradual blending commences as the printing proceeds. Bottom: Blending becomes more subtle with additional impressions.

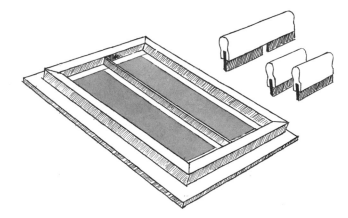

A "split fountain" arrangement makes it possible to print two or more colors at one time, if color areas are sufficiently separated. The squeegee may be one piece with splits, or separate squeegees may be used—one for each color.

prepare their own; this is usually done by screening on a white cardboard a series of narrow bands of different colors crossing each other at right angles.

Additional prerun color tests may be necessary. But, in a general way, a color chart will prove to be helpful in determining the degree of transparency, the number of colors needed, and the order in which they should be printed.

How to Print Several Colors at the Same Time

You don't always have to use different stencils for different colors. Here are some of the ways in which several colors can be printed from one stencil at the same time.

Blends and tonal effects: A wide range of tones and values can be produced by using shading sheets, as well as blends of ink directly on the screen.

☐ *Gradual blend*—The best reproducible art for screen printing, commercially speaking at least, is where each color is kept within a clearly defined boundary—poster style. It's possible, however, for limited blending effects to be achieved if the blends are gradual and follow on a parallel line in the direction of the squeegee stroke, either up and down, or side to side. Though it's impractical to blend a circular area in concentric shades, a broad background, such as a sky where the color changes in a gradual blend from a deep blue on top to a pale blue on the horizon, can be managed nicely.

To achieve the blend in the sky, you might employ three distinct shades of blue—deep blue, medium blue, and a pale blue—all of the same consistency, each mixed in its own container. Place the colors in their proper order into the screen. Select a squeegee large enough to take in all three colors at one time. The first few prints will show three distinct bands of blue. After a while, the inks in the screen will gradually run into each other, and in blending, produce a subtle airbrush-like gradation of tone. The blend will change from print to print as the inks in the screen intermix more and more. The results will be similar, but not identical. The chances are that after a dozen or so impressions, the colors will be so intermixed that the blend effect will be lost. To restore it, each of the colors in the screen must be periodically replenished. Blending, of course, is a slow process, best suited for limited editions where speed of production is of no special consequence.

(Right) The principle of the four color halftone process traditionally associated with commercial lithographic color reproduction is successfully applied in this example of a screen print made with presensitized photofilm. Courtesy Ulano Products Co., Inc., New York.

(Left) Summer Landscape, Artist's Proof, *by Andrew Stasik, courtesy the artist. This serigraph combined with lithography is printed on a 22" x 29" deckle-edged paper stock; the texture of the paper contributes appreciably to the soft quality of the finished print. The black is lithographed from a zinc plate; the colors are screen printed.*

(Above) Structured Form *by Harold Krisel, courtesy the artist. Although the edition was limited to fifty impressions, the handcut film stencils used by the artist could easily hold up for an edition running into the thousands.*

The Black Sun *by Ron Walotsky, courtesy The Dream Merchants, New York. Startling color effects are achieved with the use of luminous links screened with handcu film stencils.*

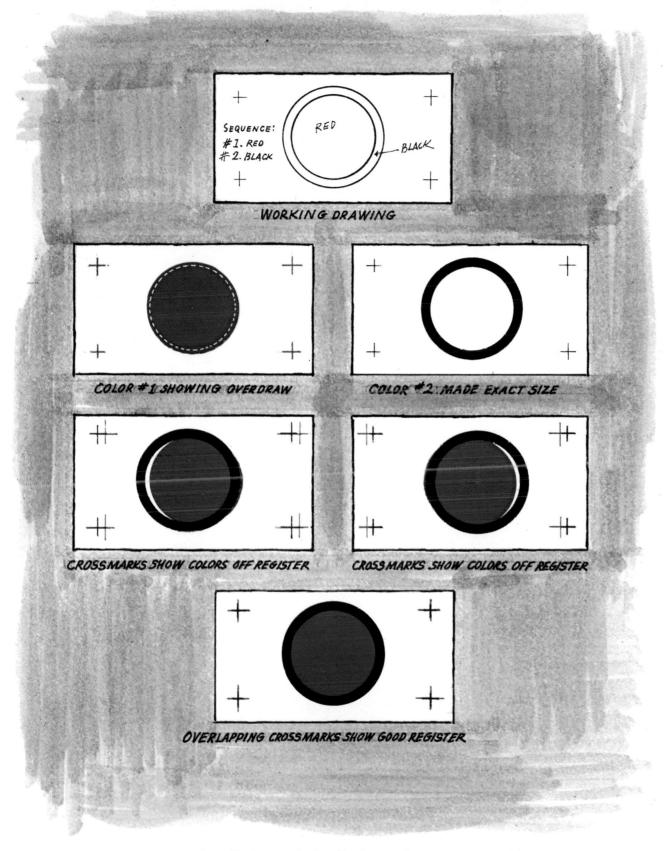

WORKING DRAWING

Sequence:
#1. RED
#2. BLACK

RED

BLACK

COLOR #1 SHOWING OVERDRAW

COLOR #2 MADE EXACT SIZE

CROSSMARKS SHOW COLORS OFF REGISTER

CROSSMARKS SHOW COLORS OFF REGISTER

OVERLAPPING CROSSMARKS SHOW GOOD REGISTER

In multicolor reproduction, it's of utmost importance to control the position of color areas as they relate to each other. The crossmarks register system, almost universally used by traditional graphic arts processes, is also applicable to screen printing. This system of color registration is exemplified here.

(Left) These progressive proofs, in the sequence in which they appear, show the development of the picture image color by color.

(Above) The completed print, from an original watercolor by Max Arthur Cohn, was screened in eight transparent colors aligned in exact register.

□ *Free mixture blend*—In the gradual blend effect just described, a smooth tonal transition was an important element in the final results achieved. With the free mixture blend, different colors are placed in the screen in what would appear to be a quite haphazard fashion. Colors can be as varied as you wish and may or may not be of the same consistency. The printing is done by squeegeeing the colors across the screen, or for that matter, in any direction. Obviously, no two prints will be the same; every impression will be an "original" print.

It's impossible to set down a precise method for achieving free mixture blends of this kind. Freedom to experiment, coupled with inventiveness and experience with the technique, can yield highly personalized effects that go beyond any prescribed course of action.

□ *Patented shading sheets*—It's possible to achieve a wide range of color values, each as a distinct tint or tone, by employing shading sheets in conjunction with photographic stencils. Thus, for example, black ink with but one printing can produce, in addition to its full strength color, a variety of tints from off-black to the palest of grays. The size and proximity of the dots on the shading sheets determine the range of tonal effects achievable.

Split fountain: Two or more colors may be printed all at the same time with the same basic screen, if the color areas are sufficiently separated from each other. In such a case, the screen is partitioned off by means of heavy cardboard strips fastened vertically to the screen and made leakproof.

Thus, each partitioned-off area can be printed either with its own fit-to-measure squeegee, or with one squeegee with a rubber blade that's slit to fit over the partitions. In this manner several colors can be printed simultaneously. This method of printing is referred to in the trade as *split fountain* printing. Its main advantage is that it saves printing time in multicolor work—a factor of practical importance where large run editions are concerned.

If the color areas are too near to each other to allow for partitions, a basic stencil incorporating several color areas may still be put into use. While one color is printed, the others are temporarily blocked out with a paper mask taped to the underside of the screen. This procedure, though it doesn't save time in printing, *does* save considerable time in stencil preparation.

The Four Color Process

Almost any art can be reproduced in an unlimited range of colors with only four printings, by employing the four color process. Here's the procedure.

The art is photographed through a series of four different color filters; each filter extracts and separates its corresponding color component—red, yellow, blue, and black. A halftone positive is prepared for each of the four colors, terminating in a set of four photographic stencils. In printing, each stencil produces the complete picture image in a dot pattern of its corresponding color. The four stencils, when printed in proper sequence and register, yield a finished print which simulates the original art in every detail and color nuance.

For all practical purposes, multicolor screen printing based on the four color process principle is, as yet, beyond the scope of the beginner or even the average practitioner in the business. Excellent results are achievable, but these results require not only a fairly high degree of technical skill in photographic controls, but also professional equipment. There are a number of photoservice houses which specialize in preparing single color and four color process screens for printers.

The Selectasine Method

With the Selectasine method (variously called the *Elimination* or *Single screen* method), it's feasible to print two, three, five, or any number of colors in a planned sequence from the same basic stencil and same makeready. A comprehensive key tracing in pen and ink is made on the screen. It incorporates all the color areas of the art, each area identified by a code number or other symbol. A master stencil is then made, leaving all design areas open. After each of the colors is printed, the image area on the master stencil corresponding to that color is blocked out, reducing the size of the open area. This blocking out continues until the last color is printed. Ink is built up on top of ink, producing a multiplane effect—an identifying characteristic of this technique.

Since with each color the basic stencil is irrevocably changed, the various steps cannot be repeated if another edition is needed. In the event of a re-run, the basic stencil would have to be made over again. Also, an inordinate amount of ink is consumed in the build-up of color. Therefore the Selectasine method is rarely used commercially, but it offers interesting possibilities for printmakers.

(Left) The adroit use of transparent inks and the sequence in which they're printed make it possible to achieve a prodigious range of color effects with a limited number of printings. This abstract composition designed by the author was produced by printing blue, red, yellow, and gray in superimposition.

Artists Proof #4 *by Lloyd Fertig, courtesy the artist. Film stencils and transparent inks were used to produce this simple but effective design.*

CHAPTER TEN

What you should know about inks and other screen printing media

Stencil making is one phase of the screen process; another is ink preparation; the third is the actual printing procedure.

At this point of our technical orientation, we're ready to proceed with the second phase, *ink preparation*. This involves selecting and mixing the right printing medium and modifying it when necessary to suit specific requirements—a task which in no small measure affects the quality of the finished print. The most perfectly executed stencil won't yield the results you seek unless the ink is right for the job on hand.

In this chapter we'll explore the various kinds of screen inks, not from the theoretic perspective of the chemist, but rather from the practical viewpoint of the printer, with special emphasis on working properties.

The word *ink* as it's used here is meant to designate categorically the entire range of printing media, and in this sense is synonomous with "paint," "color," and "process paints." These terms are often used interchangeably in dealer brochures and other commercial literature, as well as in common trade parlance.

Fifty or sixty years ago, when screen printing was in its infancy, the screen printer had to be somewhat of an amateur chemist, because ready-made screen inks weren't on the market. Often as not, he had to grind his own pigments from raw materials bought at the chemist's shop, or else make modifications of sign painter's colors, artist's oil colors, lithographer's inks—even ordinary household paints—adapting them as best as he could. By contrast, the screen printer of today can avail himself of a wide variety of ready to use inks—oil based paints, water based paints, enamels, lacquers, emulsion inks, and an ever increasing number of synthetics—all scientifically formulated under laboratory conditions.

Though modern screen ink technology has reached a high state of development (you can get all the ready-made inks you require by just picking up the phone or writing out an order) it's, nonetheless, helpful to have a basic understanding of the fundamental components of inks with particular reference to their working properties.

Fundamental Components of Inks

Simply stated, all screen inks, whether they're oil based paints, enamels, watercolors, etc., are made up of two basic components—pigment and vehicle.

The pigment: This part consists of concentrated coloring matter in the form of finely ground particles derived from minerals, plant or animal life, or evolved through synthetic processes. Irrespective of source of origin, it's the pigment which imparts the color characteristic to the ink.

Pigments differ considerably in their intrinsic color potency and tinting power. For example, phthalocyanine and oxide pigments rate high in tinting power; cadmium and earth pigments rate low.

Some pigments are far more costly to produce than others; this accounts for the rather wide range in the price of inks.

Intermixed with the pure color pigment are inert compounds, referred to in the trade as *fillers*. Fillers contribute little or no distinct color of their own. Their primary function is to serve as an additive to extend the volume of the ink mixture, quite often improving the ink's printing quality as well. Some typical inert compounds are aluminum stearate, aluminum palmitate, sodium silicate, and cornstarch. All thicken the ink mixture and increase its volume. An inordinate proportion of inerts may cause ink to become brittle, often greatly diminishing its chromatic intensity and permanence.

The vehicle: That's the fluid part of an ink; it contains a volatile solvent and a "binder" of oil, resin, or gum substance. The solvent provides the necessary flow property to render the ink adaptable for printing. Solvents in oil based inks are usually of the mineral spirits type. In lacquers, the solvents used are acetone, butyl or amyl acetate, and ethylene glycol. When the solvent evaporates, the binder remains on the printing surface to form a protective film around the pigment particles, keeping them permanently adhered to the surface.

The component ingredients in the vehicle determine the finish or surface texture, flexibility, drying time, and other working properties of the ink mixture.

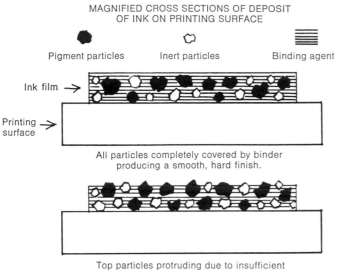

MAGNIFIED CROSS SECTIONS OF DEPOSIT
OF INK ON PRINTING SURFACE

Pigment particles   Inert particles   Binding agent

Ink film →

Printing
surface →

All particles completely covered by binder
producing a smooth, hard finish.

Top particles protruding due to insufficient
or improper binder, producing a rough, abrasive ink film.

Ink Classifications

There are many possible classifications for inks based on chemical formulation, permanence, opacity, adhesive qualities, etc. The most common classification relates to the specific principle of drying. In this context, all inks may be grouped into four major categories: inks which dry by (a) evaporation, (b) oxidation, (c) polymerization, and (d) penetration.

Inks that dry by evaporation: Inks designed to dry by evaporation include most lacquers, vinyls, and water based paints, in addition to many of today's quick drying poster inks and synthetics. In these inks drying occurs as the solvents escape into the surrounding air, leaving the pigment adhered to the surface by the action of the binder.

Drying by evaporation depends largely on the presence of units of resins or gums—film formers which are completely soluble in one or more solvents. With the evaporation of the solvents, these resins or gums combine to form a solid layer of ink. Evaporation is a purely physical change; it's reversible. This means that the dried film of ink can be redissolved with the proper solvent.

The marked characteristic of evaporating-type inks is the rapidity with which they dry on the printed surface. This, in part, accounts for their widespread use in industry where drying time is an important factor in meeting production schedules. Surprisingly enough, though they dry quickly on the printed surface, they don't dry into the screen mesh during the course of printing, nor do they *skin up* (form a surface film) in the open container.

Inks that dry by oxidation: In inks that are formulated to dry by oxidation, drying takes place in two stages: the first comes about with the physical evaporation of volatile solvents; the second involves a chemical interaction between oils in the ink and oxygen in the air.

Oxidizing inks contain fatty or "long" oils which, upon combining with oxygen, slowly and imperceptably change from a liquid to a solid state. This transition produces a new compound. A chemical reaction called *oxidation* takes place, similar in some ways to the condition which causes iron to rust. In oxidizing inks, the presence of the newly formed compounds produces a hard film which resists redissolution. The process of oxidation constitutes a "one-way" change, that is, one that isn't reversible.

Bear this in mind: with evaporating-type inks, when the solvents are totally dispersed, drying is complete. Not so with oxidizing inks. Here, the actual drying cycle is just beginning. The sooner the solvents leave the printing surface, the sooner oxidation (and drying) can start. Some of the common oxidizing oils used, singly or in combination, in the manufacture of oil based screen inks are linseed oil, soybean oil, tung oil, castor oil, otticica, and perilla. There are many more.

Oxidizing inks inherently possess excellent qualities of adhesion and permanence. These two working properties are especially important for printing on metal and glassware, outdoor signs, ceramic tiles, and similar nonabsorbent surfaces. The major drawback of oxidizing inks is their long drying time. Prints screened with enamels, and other inks that dry largely by oxidation, require eight to ten hours—sometimes overnight—to dry completely. Indeed, it would take even longer—weeks, perhaps months—if driers weren't added. Such driers as metallic salts of cobalt, lead, manganese, calcium, and zinc, through a catalytic action, help accelerate the drying process of these inks. Each salt has its own particular drying property. For example, cobalt causes the layer of ink to harden from the top down; lead works the other way—it hardens the ink from the bottom up; manganese on the other hand, activates the drying simultaneously throughout. Knowledge of these unique drying properties can be important when oxidizing inks are used in the actual printing operation. Prints which appear dry to the touch when you feel the top surface may really not be dry through and through. At least they're not dry enough to stack up without danger of sticking together.

No screen inks made today are formulated to dry solely by oxidation. Though many gloss enamels, poster colors, and other oil based inks contain oxidizing oils, they're chemicaly balanced with other ingredients to respond to evaporation, penetration, and polymerization.

Inks that dry by polymerization: In these inks drying takes place when molecular units (called polymers) of oil or resin link up in head-to-toe fashion. Thus, they form a network of solid chains which steadfastly resist further change. Once the film of ink dries, it's extremely hard, and impervious to redissolving.

In terms of end results polymerization is similar to oxidation, but polymerization takes place much faster. Since oxygen isn't a co-agent in the drying process, the ink film will dry through in a comparatively short time. Drying time can be further shortened with heat treatment. Exposure to high temperatures matures the film of ink, making it so tough that it's virtually scratch and abrasionproof. These desirable characteristics of polymerization inks, as well as their ability to bond permanently with the stock's surface, make them industrial favorites for screening on glassware, many types of plastics, outdoor metal signs, etc.

Inks that dry by penetration: In the penetration principle of drying, the inks are specifically formulated to be readily absorbed by the stock, yet retain their maximum degree of surface brilliance, flexibility, and permanence. The fluid part of the ink enters the stock by capillary action; enough resin or other type of binder remains on the surface to hold the pigment that comprises the printed image. The more absorbent the stock, the faster the degree of penetration, and the quicker drying will take place.

Penetration is usually a fast drying process—perhaps the fastest means of drying in commercial use today. It works hand in hand with evaporation; indeed, it's sometimes difficult to tell where one process ends and the other begins.

The speed of drying is the chief advantage of penetration inks. This accounts for their popularity in the production of paper signs for supermarkets, cleaning stores, and other chainstore businesses, as well as for book jackets, wallpaper, and the like. Penetration inks and dyes are especially important in the textile printing industry. Not only can the colors be made to come through to the underside of the fabric, but also the drying action starts so fast that it's possible to follow immediately with the next step in the printing sequence.

Conceivably every ink mixture can be made to penetrate an absorbent surface if sufficiently diluted. However, excessive thinning can cause the ink to change color, lose permanence, and, in some cases, to chalk or powder off. Inks scientifically developed by the manufacturer possess the right combination of selected thinning agents and other solvents, not easily duplicated in the print shop.

Don't assume that all screen inks are formulated to respond to one method of drying exclusively. The majority of inks in use today are made to dry by more than one method, and thereby benefit by the inherent advantages of all.

There are well over 500 different ingredients that go into the manufacture of today's screen inks. These include a bewildering assortment of natural and synthetic pigments, resins, gums, driers, waxes, plasticizers, extenders, oils, and solvents. It's beyond the scope of this book, or for that matter, beyond the practical needs of the average screen printer, to delve too deeply into the chemical make-up of the various lines or types of inks. It is, however, important to familiarize yourself with the major lines of inks available, with special reference to their applications and working properties.

Poster Inks

Type of stencil	Any type
Wash-up solvent	Kerosene or any of the mineral spirits
Dries mainly by	Evaporation
Normal drying time	Flat—20–30 min. Gloss—30–40 min.

Poster inks (often referred to as *process inks*) come in flat as well as in gloss finish. Unlike standard oil based formulations, which dry largely by oxidation, these inks—formulated on a modified rubber or an ethyl cellulose base—dry primarily by the process of evaporation. They dry comparatively fast; this feature makes them, by far, the most adaptable medium for general commercial use in the printing of posters and displays. Normal air drying time takes from twenty to forty minutes. However, poster inks designed for high-speed production with automatic printing presses dry in a matter of seconds with the use of coordinated drying equipment.

Inherently inclined to be opaque, poster inks may be altered to any degree of transparency with the admixture of transparent base or extender base. They may be thinned with compatible reducers. They dry with a smooth scuffproof finish, and adhere well to most surfaces except certain plastic-coated materials. Poster inks have good flexibility—an important factor to consider when the printing stock is to be folded, scored, or diecut.

Poster inks can be used with any type of stencil technique—resist, blockout, handcut film, photo, and paper. They're easy to work with, and don't pucker or curl the paper or other material on which they're printed. They're waterproof and have good permanence.

Enamel Inks

Type of stencil	Any type
Wash-up solvent	Kerosene or any of the mineral spirits
Dries mainly by	Oxidation
Normal drying time	Approx. 8–10 hrs. (or longer)

Enamels which dry by oxidation take anywhere from eight to ten hours to dry. In fact, overnight drying is recommended by most manufacturers.

Why then use enamels when poster inks dry so much faster? For one thing, enamels have an exceptionally high degree of durability, adhesiveness, and flexibility. These qualities make them a choice medium for printing on metals, ceramic tile, glassware, certain plastic and polyethylene surfaces, as well as decals. They're, of course, equally serviceable for printing on paper and cardboard stock. Then too, because of their exceptionally smooth working consistency, enamels print exceedingly sharp, usually with a slightly embossed effect. They come in an array of brilliant colors; all dry with a porcelain-like gloss finish. When dry these enamels retain almost the same rich depth of color that they possess when wet.

Many enamels are of the "cold" variety, that is, they require no heat treatment. There are, however, special baking enamels intended for firing at temperatures ranging from 275° to 350° F. The firing process makes the printed surface virtually scratchproof.

Enamel inks can be used with all stencil methods, but special care must be taken in washing the screen. Any vestige of ink that's allowed to dry into the mesh is almost impossible to remove at a later time.

Printing with enamels is reserved for "special" jobs since they're comparatively expensive. Their prices range from 30%–50% above that of standard poster inks.

Lacquer Inks

Type of stencil	Any type except those with a lacquer base
Wash-up solvent	Lacquer thinner
Dries mainly by	Evaporation
Normal drying time	Industrial—40–60 min. Decal—1–2 hrs.

There are many brands, but essentially there are only two main types: industrial lacquers and decal lacquers.

Industrial lacquers are used mostly for screening on pyroxylin-coated material, though they work equally well on metallic foils, paper, cardboard, and other conventional printing surfaces. They air-dry in forty to sixty minutes. Drying time can be drastically cut with the use of mechanical drying equipment, either circulating air, heat, or both.

Decal lacquers (sometimes referred to as *flexible* lacquers), while primarily developed for printing decalcomanias (decals, for short), can also be used for paper or cardboard, or for that matter on any surface where a smooth, flexible film is required. Decal lacquers generally contain a large proportion of finely ground solids; these ingredients endow

them with superior color permanence and adhesiveness. They take considerably longer to dry, but in all other respects respond to the same handling as industrial lacquers.

Both types have this in common: they dry by evaporation; both require lacquer resistant stencils. Also both employ a blend of lacquer thinners as a reducer and as a solvent for washing screens and squeegees. They also share this limitation: because of their strong toxic banana oil odor, they're not easy to work with in close quarters. At home, studio, or classroom adequate ventilation must be provided through an exhaust or other efficient air-flow system. Discretion must also be exercised when smoking or working near an open flame, since lacquers catch fire even more easily than oil based inks.

Lacquers made for screen printing are available in several finishes: gloss, semigloss, and high gloss. Colors—and there's a great range of them—are, for the most part, fairly opaque as they come in the container. However, like all screen inks, they may be modified to any degree of transparency by adding clear base.

As an adjunct to the regular line of opaques, ready-mixed transparent lacquers formulated with pigments of high color intensity are available for printing on aluminum foil. These produce a luminous metallic sheen, an effect heightened by the natural reflective surface of the foil. Lacquers are also made to be acid resistant, when this working property is an industrial requirement, as in the case of printed circuits. Such lacquers (principally black) are used in the electronics industry. They're not affected by ferric chloride or similar etching solutions.

When printing with lacquer inks, it's imperative to make tests on the actual surface to which the ink will be applied. This is especially true when the surface happens to be pyroxylin or other plastic material. Lacquers usually possess excellent adhesion for most surfaces, including a great variety of plastics. However, the chemistry of plastics is so complex that differences in surface characteristics, though imperceptible to the eye, can make one plastic compatible with lacquer and another incompatible with it.

Vinyl Inks

Type of stencil	Any type except those with a lacquer base
Wash-up solvent	Lacquer thinner
Dries mainly by	Evaporation
Normal drying time	Flat—3–5 min. Gloss—10–15 min.

Designed primarily for printing on vinyl surfaces (flexible or rigid), these inks air-dry by evaporation within fifteen minutes, depending upon type of finish, weather conditions, and ventilation. In some cases, heat may be applied to accelerate drying and to complete the fusion of ink and stock. Vinyl inks are durable and possess a propensity for physically fusing with the printing surface. For these reasons they're extensively used for screening on shower curtains, vinyl-coated wallpaper, and plastic tablecloths. They are also used for screening on cosmetic containers, plastic toys, inflatable balloons, decorative umbrellas and rainwear, and any other items where the printed design becomes an integral part of the stock.

Vinyl inks are formulated to print in a range of different finishes, from flat to gloss. They come opaque in the container, but may be reduced to practically any degree of transparency by the addition of a special base. In some colors—black, for example—the reduction may be as high as 50% without seriously affecting color identity or coverage. Vinyl inks can be thinned to a much more fluid consistency than standard poster inks without a loss of sharpness or image clarity.

One of the unique working properties of vinyl inks is that, though they dry rapidly *on* the printing surface, they don't dry *into* the screen, even if the printer stops for lunch, leaving the screen unattended. No wash-ups for short recesses are necessary. Washing up at the end of the day is done with lacquer thinner, the same that's used for lacquer inks.

As far as stencils are concerned, any stencil technique which produces a lacquer resistant stencil tissue can be used. Photographic stencils, especially those made with the direct method, are best when long runs are anticipated.

When printing with vinyl inks as with lacquer inks, proper ventilation to remove the build-up of toxic fumes is necessary. Fire precautions must be strictly observed because of the inflammable nature of both the inks and the solvents.

In all cases, before proceeding with the production run, trial tests should be made on the actual surface to be printed to assure compatibility between ink and stock.

Acrylic Inks

Type of stencil	Any type except those with a lacquer base
Wash-up solvent	Lacquer thinner
Dries mainly by	Evaporation and polymerization
Normal drying time	40–60 min.

Acrylic inks are chemically formulated on a resin base similar to that of the plastic surfaces on which they're printed. These include rigid acetate, many of the phenolics and polystyrenes, Plexiglas, Lucite, and related synthetics encompassed in the broad family of plastics. Compatibility between ink and printing surface assures maximum adhesion and durability—two important qualities which make acrylic inks especially adaptable for screening on stock designed for vacuum forming fabrication.

Under normal room temperature, acrylic inks dry within thirty to fifty minutes; within thirty seconds or less, if subjected to heat treatment at temperatures ranging from 190° to 210° F. Colors dry with a satin gloss finish and with a moderate degree of opacity. Manufacturers prepare acrylic inks so that, in most instances, they may be used directly from the container; however, compatible thinners are available for reducing the viscosity of the ink when a more fluid mixture is desired.

When working with acrylic inks, the stencils must be lacquer resistant. This excludes handcut lacquer film stencils or blockout stencils made with a lacquer medium. Also, it's important to remember that pretesting of ink on an actual sample of the plastic to be printed is a precaution that *should not* be ignored. An efficient system of ventilation is mandatory, because of the volatile nature of the ink and the toxicity of built-up fumes.

Epoxy Inks

Type of stencil	Any type except those with a lacquer base
Wash-up solvent	Lacquer thinner
Dries mainly by	Polymerization
Normal drying time	Tack free—3 hrs. Fully dry—7–10 days

A polymerizing ink with unsurpassed adhesive properties for printing on glass, metal, and thermosetting plastics, epoxy inks are reserved almost exclusively for industrial purposes. They're hardly ever used for advertising. In view of their extreme resistance to acids, alkalis, solvents, and erosive chemicals, they're extensively used in the container decorating field where their durability and resistive properties are particularly advantageous. They're also widely used in the electronic, aircraft, and automobile industries for printing permanent markings on circuit boards, dials, instrument panels, and numerous other components.

Epoxy inks are unique; unlike standard inks they don't come in ready to use form. Instead they're put up in two-package units, with each container of color accompanied by a container of catalyst. The ink is prepared by the printer, about a half hour before it's needed by combining specified amounts of catalyst with color. Once mixed, the batch of ink has a pot life of no more than five or six hours. After this time a hardening action takes place, limiting its further use as a printing medium. It's not practical, therefore, to prepare more ink than is needed within that period of time. The catalyst itself will, if tightly sealed, keep for several months without spoiling, whereas the color will last almost indefinitely.

Only lacquer resistant stencils can be used, and these must be cleaned immediately after printing with lacquer thinner and prior to the end of the ink's pot life. Even the slightest hardening of the ink in the screen will create a serious problem in cleaning and wash-up.

Prints screened with epoxy inks dry by air or by baking, depending upon the type of catalyst used. Either way drying, or "curing" as it's called, continues for days, long after the prints are surface dry. When curing is complete, maximum adhesion and permanence are achieved.

Aqua (Tempera) Colors

Type of stencil	Any type except those with a water base
Wash-up solvent	Water
Dries mainly by	Evaporation and penetration
Normal drying time	5–10 min.

Water based tempera colors, the kind artists use for posters and showcards, dry much too fast to be practical for screen printing. After two or three impressions, artists' tempera colors dry into the mesh of the screen. This condition can be partially overcome by adding glycerin or honey to the colors to serve as a retarder. The easy availability of special tempera colors, marketed as Aqua colors, designed for screen printing makes such remedial measures unnecessary.

Aqua colors are comparitively odorless, contain no flammable solvents, and air-dry rapidly on the printed surface, eliminating extensive racking facilities. Since the colors are water-soluble, screen and squeegee are easily cleaned with ordinary tap water. While, undeniably, these constitute decided advantages, Aqua colors have but limited application in commercial screen printing. There are a number of reasons why: the colors (though brilliant) lack opacity, making it difficult for a light color to cover a dark one. The inherent transparency of the color can, of course, be exploited as an advantage if additional color effects are judiciously planned through overprinting. But generally speaking, Aqua colors don't allow comparable opportunities for controlling the degree of opacity as do oil based or lacquer based inks.

Perhaps a more serious drawback to Aqua colors is that they're not waterproof and, therefore, can't be considered for printed materials intended for outdoor exposure. Also they lack the adhesive quality necessary for stock *other* than paper, cardboard, and similar absorbent surfaces.

Within the range of these technical limitations, Aqua colors, nonetheless, offer many compensatory features of special significance to the noncommercial screen printer for home, studio, and classroom.

Emulsion-type Textile Inks
Oil based

Type of stencil	Any type, but direct photo screen is best
Wash-up solvent	Kerosene or any of the mineral spirits
Dries mainly by	Evaporation
Normal drying time	30–40 min.

Water based

Type of stencil	Any type except those with a water base
Wash-up solvent	Water
Dries mainly by	Evaporation and penetration
Normal drying time	10–20 min.

Emulsion-type inks (principally used for screening on fabrics) are made by mixing a clear emulsion with a highly concentrated color pigment or toner. The basic emulsion is produced by dissolving a resin in a solvent. Then, through homogenization, it's combined with water and/or mineral spirits. The resin acts as the binding agent for the pigment particles; the solvent evaporates in drying. Emulsion-type inks may be formulated as water based or oil based mixtures depending upon production requirements.

It's possible to get emulsion-type inks in ready-mixed colors; better results, however, are achieved if the concentrated pigment and the clear emulsion are bought separately and combined with a high-speed mixer as needed. The ratio of pigment to clear emulsion is governed by the degree of color intensity desired. By nature transparent, emulsion-type inks yield maximum chromatic intensity when printed on white or light colored surfaces. Where a degree of opacity is required, a special white opaque ink can be added without seriously affecting the original color value.

Fabrics printed with emulsion-type inks usually require washing, steaming, or other curing treatments to set the color and assure permanence and flexibility.

Luminescent Inks

In the broad category of luminescent inks are included the daylight fluorescent inks, the so-called blacklight fluorescents which must be activated by an ultraviolet light source, and the industrial phosphorescents. Of these, the daylight fluorescent-type ink is, by far, the most popular.

Daylight fluorescent inks: Sold under such trade names as DayGlo, Radiant Color, and VelvaGlo, these special screen inks have a chromatic intensity four to five times greater than conventional inks. They have a built-in capability to absorb the ultraviolet energy of sunlight or artificial light. They convert this energy to a visible color spectrum so bright as to give the illusion of being illuminated from within.

Daylight fluorescent inks contain millions of glasslike high spectrum particles of pigment solubilized in specially treated resins. Inherently transparent, they must be printed on white stock to retain their maximum brilliance. They come in a limited palette of colors: red, tangerine, pink, cerise, orange, yellow, green, chartreuse, and blue. Red, orange, and yellow are commercially the most widely used, because they're the brightest of the lot. This is especially true if surrounded by a black, deep blue, or other dark-hued conventional ink. Colors can't be intermixed to get compound colors; each must be used as it comes in the container. However, the color may be modified in consistency with a compatible thinning agent or plasticizer.

Exposed outdoors in direct sunlight, these inks retain their brilliance for twenty to thirty days, after which they fade rapidly. Indoors, they stand up for much longer periods of time—sometimes for years. Effective applications of daylight fluorescent inks are evident in brightly colored greeting cards, posters and displays, billboards, textile prints, identification markings on aircraft, and to some extent in serigraphic art.

Blacklight fluorescent inks: The unique character of these inks is that when viewed in the dark under "blacklight" conditions, they take on a phantom-like radiance unmatched in brilliance by any other type of ink. Blacklight, usually in the form of a high-pressure mercury arc lamp or a special low-pressure fluorescent tube covered with a cobalt blue filter, emits a concentration of near-ultraviolet rays. It's these rays which activate the fluorescent pigments in the ink. Blacklight fluorescent inks are available in a select range of colors; green and yellow are the most popular, since they possess unsurpassed luminosity.

The most extensive use of blacklight fluorescent inks is in the screen printing of instrument dials for airplanes, automobiles, radios, etc. They're also used in the production of novelty posters and billboard advertising.

Phosphorescent inks: Commonly known as luminous paints, phosphorescent inks glow in total darkness only. They absorb any kind of light and store it up, much like a storage battery stores up electricity; they then release this light energy as an afterglow in the dark when the original light source has been removed. This light emission property of phosphorescent inks can be reactivated to capacity over and over again, without diminishing the phosphorescent potency of the pigment.

Phosphorescent inks come in a rather limited color range: light orange, yellow, green, and blue. Afterglow varies from one half to two hours for the orange, yellow, and green, while blue retains its glow up to ten hours. Pigment and vehicle are supplied in separate containers, and only enough is mixed to take care of immediate use.

Both phosphorescent and "blacklight" inks have a strong, pungent odor. Unless exceptionally good ventilation is provided, neither type lends itself to extensive printing projects. Commercially, phosphorescent inks are employed for shelter signs, wall plaques, instrument dials, military charts, and components for computers.

Note: Luminescent inks are produced in oil, water, and various lacquer formulations. Therefore the selection of the stencil techniques and their compatible wash-up solvents will depend on the particular formulation of luminescent ink used.

Metallic Inks

These come in a stabilized ready-mixed form intended to be used straight from the container, as well as in powder form to be mixed with a vehicle prior to printing. The latter, to retain its full luster, must be used the same day as it's prepared.

The pigments in metallic inks, called *lining bronzes,* are ground exceedingly fine in order to go through the mesh of the screen. The vehicle may be oil, lacquer, or water based and includes an effective binding agent to keep the metallic pigment permanently anchored to the printing surface. Properly prepared, metallic inks will dry with a smooth, hard finish and retain their metallic luster for a very long time. The choice of colors includes several shades of gold, silver, and copper. All have excellent opacity and can be screened onto any surface compatible with the vehicle.

Special Compounds

The screen process lends itself not only to printing with a variety of ink formulations, but also to the mechanical application of adhesives, glass etching compounds, conductive paints and resists used in printed circuits, and any other viscous compounds that can be squeegeed through the screen mesh.

Adhesive compounds: With varying degrees of success, any type of oil based paint, lacquer, or other

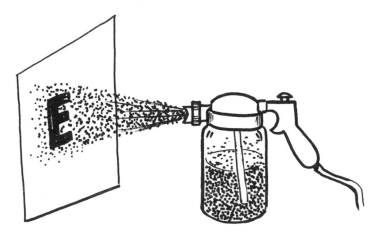

Flock may be applied to the adhesive surface in many ways depending upon facilities and production requirements. One way is to make use of a flock spray gun such as the one shown here.

For limited editions flock may be applied with a coarse sieve.

standard ink can serve as an adhesive compound for flock and similar appliqué effects. However, commercial printers engaged mainly in flocking almost always show a preference for ready-mixed screen adhesives. These adhesives are formulated to possess the right degree of tack, holding power, and flexibility. Screen adhesives are manufactured in transparent form or in opaque form to match the color of the appliqué.

Adhesive compounds are screened with the same equipment and in the same manner as printing inks. They're available not only for flock, but also for tinsel material, such as fine glass glitter, crushed acetate or aluminum flakes, and mother-of-pearl dust simulating ice, snow, and other reflective textures. Irrespective of its nature or composition, once the appliqué material has settled and become embedded in the tacky surface of the adhesive-printed stock, the surplus is shaken off, or in some other way removed. When dry, the adhesive creates a permanent bond between appliqué and stock.

Screening with adhesives is a routine operation in the production of flocked wallpaper, banners, pennants, T-shirts, velour linings for jewelry cases, as well as for glitter effects on posters, window displays, and novelty greeting cards.

In addition, it's possible to screen gold size adhesive, the kind sign painters use for applying pure gold, silver, and other metal leaf on plate glass and wood panels. The size is screened onto the receiving surface, and when it reaches the required degree of tack, the leaf is laid down by hand in the traditional manner of the craft.

Glass etching compounds: There are several methods by which an etched or a frosted effect may be produced on glassware with the use of screen stencils; there are ready-made preparations for each method. One involves an acid resist compound such as asphaltum. The compound is screened onto the surface of the glass, leaving the area to be etched open. An all-over coating of the compound is then applied to the *back* as well as to the *edges* of the glass. When immersed in an acid bath, only the exposed *(open)* area of the glass is affected, the resist compound being impervious to the action of the acid. Upon dissolving the resist compound, the etched area emerges in sharp contrast to the rest of the glass. This method can also be used on mirrored surfaces. The acid will dissolve any area of the silver backing not protected by the resist compound.

Another method for achieving an etched effect is considerably simpler; it's used where a surface frosting rather than a deep etch is desired. It's a direct rather than a resist method, thus eliminating the need for an acid bath. An aqueous paste mixture of a fluoride compound, resembling a colorless jelly, is screened onto the surface of a glass in the same manner as conventional inks. The printed area is allowed to set for several minutes, after which the glass is washed with running water to stop further chemical action. When the glass is dry, the design appears as a uniform frosted area, permanent and indelible.

A feature of this glass etching compound is that with casual contact it's noninjurious to hands. It's easy to work with, and requires no special equipment. The compound is water-soluble, and can be applied with any type of waterproof stencil.

Inks and resist compounds for printed circuits: The printing of electronic circuits has been made possible with the formulation of special metallic inks which embody the ingredients necessary to transmit an electric current. The inks are mixtures of finely ground powders of a conductive metal suspended in a compatible vehicle. They screen as easily as standard poster inks, and come in various formulations directly related to the technical requirements of the particular job. In addition, there are resist compounds especially made for the etching and plating methods used in the production of screen printed circuits.

For a more detailed treatment of how these inks and resist compounds are used, see Chapter 15.

The following chart should help you in selecting a particular ink that's compatible to the specific job on hand.

Ink Selector Chart

Relative suitability of ink to stock: F = Fair; G = Good; E = Excellent

STOCK	POSTER INKS	ENAMEL INKS	LACQUER INKS	VINYL INKS	ACRYLIC INKS	EPOXY INKS	AQUA (TEMPERA) COLORS	EMULSION INKS
Paper	E	F	F		Γ		G	F
Cardboard	E	F	F		F		G	F
Foil paper		G	E	G				
Corrugated board	E	F	F				G	
Decal paper		F	E					
Glass	F	E	F		F	E		
Metal	F	E	F		F	E		
Wood	G	E	F		F			
Masonite	G	E	G		F			
Formica		E	F		F	Γ		
Felt	F	E						
Cork	G	E	F			F		
Leather	F	G	E	F				
Oilcloth	F	F	G					
Washable fabrics								E
Canvas	F	E	F					
Drill cloth	F	F	E	F	F			
Rubber		E		F				
Vinyl				E	F			
Pyroxylin-coated cloth			E	G				
Plexiglas		G	E	G	E	E		
Lucite		G	E	G	E	G		
Polyethylene		E	F		E	G		
Polystyrene	F	G			E	E		
Polyester		E						
Acetate		E	F		F			
Ceramic tile		G	F			E		

Note: Testing of ink on the stock to be printed is a procedure universally recommended by ink manufacturers.

CHAPTER ELEVEN

Mixing and matching colors

It's good to be *au courant* with the wide assortment of printing media available to the screen printer today. But it's hardly necessary—at least when you're just starting out—to equip yourself with more than a minimum working inventory. For all-around versatility and ease of handling, the modified rubber or ethyl cellulose poster inks are recommended. They can be used with any stencil method, and offer the greatest latitude in printing surfaces. Moderately opaque, they're easily made transparent with the addition of a base. Drying mainly by evaporation, they air-dry rapidly with a flat finish. Once you've acquired a good working knowledge of this line of ink, the experience gained is readily adaptable to the other printing media described in the previous chapter.

Your Initial Color Inventory

With poster inks (as in most other types of screen inks) you'll find that ink manufacturers issue color charts with spectacular arrays of twenty-five to thirty different colors and shades. Even after you've turned "pro" the chances are you won't require all of these. But the neophyte, especially, will require only a limited number of basic colors. You can, in most instances, achieve the others through intermixing. Primrose yellow and peacock blue, in proper proportion, will produce bright green; peacock blue and cerise will produce purple; yellow and red will produce orange, and so on. The matching and mixing procedures here described while referring particularly to one line of ink, namely, poster inks of the modified rubber or ethyl cellulose variety, are adaptable with some variations to other lines of ink.

An initial color inventory might consist of the following:

Lemon yellow
Yellow ochre
Mineral orange
Fire red
Cerise
Peacock blue
Ultramarine blue
White
Black

As to quantity, that naturally will vary with the extent of your printing operation. To start off experimentally (and based on plans for limited editions), a quart of each should suffice. However, since black and white are used not only as basic colors, but also for tinting and shading, it would be well to get at least a half gallon of each.

You'll also want to include a gallon of transparent base for use as an additive when transparent tints are needed; two quarts of reducing varnish for general thinning purposes; and two quarts of extender base to make the ink mixture thicker, if it's been inadvertently mixed too thin. Incidentally, transparent base and extender base are popular additives, since they cost considerably less than standard inks. As you enlarge the range of your inventory, you'll probably want to get several "toner" colors. Toners are concentrated inks in heavy paste form. They're never used by themselves, but rather in conjunction with transparent base to produce transparencies.

This about completes your initial inventory except for solvents for washing the screen and squeegee. These may be kerosene, Varnolene, turpentine, Varsol, or any of the mineral spirits. Kerosene is the least expensive of the lot and does a good job.

We'll discuss solvents, toners, and bases a bit more fully later in the chapter. Right now, let's proceed with how to go about matching and mixing colors, and how to estimate the amount you'll need for a particular job under given conditions.

Color Matching

In the main, color matching is a visual process. Although spectrographic laboratory devices are employed by ink manufacturers for scientific color matching, the average screen printer relies solely on the accuracy of visual perception to match his colors.

Wherever possible, color should be matched during the day under normal daylight conditions, but never in direct sunlight; north light is usually best. If artificial illumination is unavoidable, the use of fluorescent or daylight bulbs is preferable. Ordinary incandescent bulbs produce a yellowish cast making accurate color matching difficult.

But even under the best of lighting conditions it's not always easy to discern and match a critical color value in multicolor art, since, visually, neighboring colors tend to influence each other. This optical phenomenon is explained by the "law of simultaneous contrast" which, in effect, states that colors are influenced in hue by adjacent colors. Each imparts to its neighbor a tinge or cast of its own complement, that is, its opposite on the color wheel. For example, a red area adjacent to an area of green makes the red appear redder and the green greener.

In color matching, a good way to eliminate the influence of surrounding colors is to make use of "window cut-outs." This is easily done. Cut the same size opening in two index cards, creating a small window in each. Place one window over a swatch of the mixed color, the other over the color of the art that you want to match. By this means, both colors can be compared under the same conditions.

Window cut-outs come in handy for comparing color matches.

Procedure for Pretesting Color

A dab of color smeared on a scrap of paper doesn't constitute a reliable color match, no matter how closely it may visually approach the color on the art. The best assurance that the color is matched correctly is to check a printed sample. The following procedure, which applies specifically to opaque inks, is recommended and is one that is routine in most professional shops. The procedure for working with transparent inks is a bit more involved, because it must also take into account color changes due to overprinting.

1: Mix a small batch of ink with all the proper components, visually matching the color as closely as possible.

2: Then run a sample through a small test screen, preferably one made of the identical screen fabric used in the full-size production screen. To be a true test, color proofing should be done on a piece of the actual edition stock. The nature and color of the stock constitute determining factors in the final results.

3: Next allow the printed color swatch to dry. Many a color appears less bright when dry, and often takes on a different cast entirely.

4: Now compare the color swatch with the corresponding color on the art, making use of the window cut-out described previously.

5: Make as many revisions in the color mixture as necessary, each time retesting the results.

6: Even though the colors, as a rule, remain fairly constant once properly mixed, check the color from time to time while the job is in production. Printed results may be affected by variations in squeegee pressure and changes in ink viscosity. To maintain color uniformity throughout the edition, it's helpful

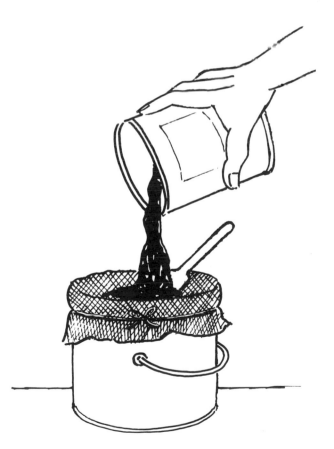

Cheesecloth securely tied over the top of a container makes a good ink strainer. A wood paddle or spoon expedites the straining operation.

to set aside one print to serve as a standard color guide and refer to it periodically.

Besides serving as an aid to color matching, pretesting offers a number of peripheral advantages. It reveals the working consistency of the ink mixture in terms of viscosity and flow, as well as the length of time it takes the ink to dry. Most important, it establishes the degree of compatibility between the ink and the printing surface, particularly with regard to adhesion and flexibility. A surface with a plastic, wax, or other chemical coating (though invisible to the naked eye) may reject the ink when it dries, resulting in scuffing, flaking, or peeling. This could be a very costly mistake in large production runs. For certain special industrial purposes (for example, printing on containers meant for perfumes, hair sprays, and cosmetics) pretesting, among other things, determines the resistance of the ink to the action of alcohols which comprise a major ingredient of the products stored in such containers.

Duplicating the Formula in Bulk

Guided by the results of the sampling tested, you're now ready to duplicate the formula in bulk quantity. When mixing inks, there are a number of things to bear in mind which apply to the preparation of the sample batch, as well as to the bulk mixture.

First and foremost, to assure complete intermixability, the pigments, bases, reducers, and other ink modifiers added to the ink mixture must be those recommended by the manufacturer for his specific line of ink products.

Metal cans, and other containers used for ink mixtures, must be clean. Inks (even if dry), left over in cans from previous runs, may discolor what otherwise would be a perfect color match. You may buy new cans cheaply enough from any paint or hardware store. They're available in sizes from a pint to a gallon and up. Avoid using cardboard containers. Solvents in inks have a way of seeping through the walls of paper-made containers causing the ink mixture to alter its original consistency. Often it brings about a change in color as well.

The ink mixture must be stirred thoroughly. Components not completely interspersed will show up in the print as flecks, streaks, or other irregularities. To achieve proper mixture, large commercial shops often use mechanical whirlers in preparing sizable batches of ink. For sample preparation and for limited production, a good stirring with a stick, spoon, or paddle is quite sufficient.

Ink should be strained if it shows any semblance of skinning, sedimentation, or other impurities. Straining may be a time-consuming task, but it's the only way to reclaim ink which contains extraneous matter. Straining can be done either with a double layer of cheesecloth tied securely around the rim of the container, or by using a fine meshed sieve.

When intermixing two (or more) colors, it's advisable to start with the lighter of the color components and add the deeper color as needed. For example, when combining red and black to produce brown, start with the red (the lighter of the two values) and add black (the darker value). A true anecdote in which I was an ingenuous participant will help to dramatize the wisdom of this council.

As a young assistant in a screen shop many years ago, I was assigned the job of preparing a gallon of gray. In the knowledge that gray was a mixture of black and white, I began with a little over half a gallon of black and proceeded to add white. Noting no marked change in color, I added more and more white until the can was full to the brim. Since the color was still much too dark (and needing additional container space), I transferred the entire contents into a five-gallon can. I continued to add white in greater and greater quantities, and with increasing anxiety. The ink in the big can was now approaching the top, and the gray wasn't nearly light enough. Instead of starting all over again (as I should have), and in my desire to retrieve the color I had been spoiling, I ultimately ended up with more than six gallons of gray before the mixture finally approached the desired shade.

Estimating the Amount of Ink Needed for a Specific Job

The experienced printer is usually able to estimate the anticipated consumption of ink with a fair degree of accuracy. In doing so, he takes into consideration the following factors.

Number of copies to be printed: Obviously, the larger the edition, the greater, proportionately, the amount of ink required.

Printing area to be covered: Complete all-over coverage will use up more ink that a limited area involving design or lettering.

Type of surface to be printed: Comparatively absorbent stock such as paper, cardboard, cloth, cork, and wood will use up more ink per square foot of printing surface than glass, metal, or other nonabsorbent material.

Size of the screen mesh: A #8 or #10 mesh deposits a heavier coat of ink than a #12 or higher; consequently, ink consumption will be greater with a coarser mesh than with a finer one.

Thickness of the stencil tissue: A stencil cut from heavy paper or film tissue deposits a correspondingly heavy coat of ink, and therefore more ink will be required.

Condition and type of squeegee rubber used: More ink is consumed when printing with a blunt, soft squeegee than when printing with one that's sharp-edged and resilient.

Pressure exerted on the squeegee: A comparatively light pressure on the squeegee (which lays down a heavy deposit of ink) will use up more ink than a firm pressure.

Within the framework of these variables, a gallon of ink will cover anywhere from 800 to 1,200 square feet of printing surface, 1,000 square feet being a convenient average. (In singular instances, as when printing on certain open-weave cloth and other highly absorbent surfaces, the anticipated coverage can be as little as 500 square feet per gallon.)

Here's a hypothetical problem. How do you estimate the amount of ink needed for an edition of 200 copies, printed solid in one color, on 18″ x 24″ posterboard?

Compute the area of the printing stock in square inches: 18″ × 24″ = 432 sq. in. Multiply the number of cards in the edition (200) by 432, to get the total number of square inches of printing surface: 432 sq. in. × 200 = 86,400 sq. in. Converting this to square feet, 86,400 divided by 144 (the number of square inches per foot), gives you a total of 600 sq. ft. for the edition. On the basis of 1,000 sq. ft. of coverage per gallon, it will take 0.6 gallon of ink to do the job.

Because of the variables affecting ink consumption alluded to before, it's generally a good idea to prepare 10%–15% more than the computed estimate. There's nothing quite as frustrating as to discover you're out of ink before the end of the edition, and you have to stop and match and mix additional ink to be able to complete the run.

Ink Modifiers

A good many screen inks on the market today are formulated to be used practically straight out of the container. There are, however, modifiers available in the form of bases, toners, solvents, and reducers, which enable the printer to adjust the basic ink formulations to the special needs of the job.

Transparent base: This is a fluffy, vaseline-like substance composed of such colloidal clays as aluminum stearate, aluminum palmitate, or bentonite, ground in the same vehicle as the ink. Transparent base serves two main functions in ink mixing: (1) it increases the transparency of the ink, and (2) it adds body and "shortness" to ink that's too free flowing. In addition, transparent base adds a lubricant quality, improving the working consistency of the ink. Because it's considerably less expensive than standard ink, transparent base is sometimes employed as an additive or filler to increase the ink volume, thus cutting down costs.

Extender base: A modified form of transparent base, extender base is used mainly as a low-cost filler to increase the volume of ink. Extender base averages about one third the price of standard inks and may frequently be used in lieu of transparent base.

For some purposes, where finish and color permanence are not crucial, extender base can be safely added to ink in a 1:3 ratio, that is, one part base to three parts ink. A larger proportion of base will cause the ink to become mealy, and appreciably lower its chromatic intensity.

Cornstarch: Ordinary household cornstarch, used in moderation, can serve as a practical expediency for thickening the ink mixture and making it "short," when neither transparent base nor extender base is available. Use discretion when adding starch. Too much starch will rob the ink of its true color qualities, reduce flexibility, and clog the screen mesh.

Toners: They're formulated with the same rich pigments and vehicles as artists' high quality oil paints. Toners (which come in more than twenty-five distinct colors) can be used to intensify the chromatic value of standard inks. Toners function mainly, however, as concentrates. Added to base, they produce transparent color values. Combined with a crystal clear base, toners permit the utmost latitude in the preparation of transparent colors. Toners may also be mixed with standard white inks to produce a full spectrum of opaque pastels.

In their natural state, toners are much too gummy and thick to be added to bases or other ink mixtures, without first being diluted with varnish, oil, or a similar reducing agent.

It's impossible to tell the true color value of a toner by the way it looks in its original paste form or even in its mixed state; the color looks ten times as dark in the container as it does in the print. The only way to check the true color value of a toner is to make a test print through the screen.

Because toners are colors of high concentration, they're capable of producing distinct shades, even when mixed as one part toner to fifty or more parts of white ink or transparent base. That's the equivalent of about a jigger of pure toner to a gallon of mixed ink. Good toners are expensive, but a little goes a long way.

Solvents: Though solvents are considered primarily as washing and cleaning fluids, they may be—and frequently are—used as ink modifiers as well. In oil based inks, compatible mineral spirits and other solvents can, with limitations, serve as thinning agents to reduce the viscosity of the ink mixture. These are, however, at best, only substitutes for regular reducers.

There are pitfalls to watch for when using solvents as thinning agents for oil based inks. Solvents can easily disturb the fine chemical balance built into the ink formulation by the manufacturer. Kerosene, for example, added to ink will undoubtedly thin it, but, at the same time, it may greatly—and sometimes unpredictably—retard drying. Turpentine, benzene, naphtha, or other highly volatile solvents, on the other hand, can produce the opposite effect, causing the ink to dry into the screen. Perhaps the safest of the solvents for general use as thinning agents are such mineral spirits as Varsol and Varnolene.

A metal can for depositing ink saturated rags is an important safety measure.

A simple card system helps keep track of the inks you have on hand.

They're neutral and don't appreciably alter the chemical balance of the ink.

Reducers: A reducer has many uses. First, it can act as a diluent to thin the ink mixture to a more fluid, working consistency. Some reducers do that and nothing more. Others are introduced to the ink mixture to slow up drying, and thus prevent clogging the screen. Still others are added to control the finish. Each is formulated by the manufacturer to serve a specific function.

Generally speaking, the reducer in oil based inks is varnish, whereas in lacquers the reducer is a species of acetone or lacquer thinner. Reducers (or, for that matter, very few printing inks) are hardly ever called by their chemical designations, but rather by a proprietary name or serial number assigned to them by the manufacturers. Thus you'll find reducers listed in the various catalogs as #569, K-1, Satin Fin, R-4B, etc.

You needn't, at this time, be overly concerned about trade names or other arbitrary designations. Your screen process supplier will provide you with data sheets and charts. These will list by name or number, not only reducers, but other modifiers, as well as his complete line of inks and printing media.

Hints on Maintaining and Storing Inks

Organizational ability and good housekeeping habits are important factors in the proper maintenance and storage of inks and related supplies. Here are some helpful hints.

Identify leftover ink mixtures with a label showing a screened swatch of the color. Also indicate the amount, its component ingredients, when the color was mixed, and for what job. This information will come in handy in the event of a re-run at some future date, or if the ink mixture is to serve as a nucleus for other colors.

Although many of today's inks don't skin up readily, it's a good shop rule to keep all inks covered, especially if they're stored for any length of time. This rule applies even more so to lacquer thinner, benzene, naphtha, and other solvents which are highly volatile and present a potential fire hazard. Provisions should be made for storing inventories of inks and solvents in steel cabinets. In many localities, fire department regulations make this mandatory. Solvent and ink-saturated rags should always be placed in self-closing metal containers, to avoid the possibility of spontaneous combustion.

It's imprudent—and a waste of valuable shelf space besides—to keep on buying more inks simply because you don't have a quick way of knowing what you have on hand. To discipline yourself in this respect, you can devise a running inventory. It can be based on a movable card system such as the one shown. In this way, each color in your stock of inks is represented by an individual card showing a color swatch, special formula (if any), manufacturer's trade name or serial number, quantity on hand, and other relevant data. For this system to be effective, the color cards should be updated periodically.

The great variety of color charts, catalogs, and data sheets issued by ink manufacturers provide an excellent source of information on standard lines of screen printing media, as well as new technical developments in the field. This material, which is generally free for the asking, can form the basis of an active and valuable reference file.

This is a good time to remind you to be selective in choosing a supplier. Once you've done so, and if his products and services meet with your complete satisfaction, it's best to stay with him. His needn't be the largest company in the field, but merely one which merits your full confidence. By dealing with one reliable company, you'll establish a good working relationship; you'll get personal attention when you require the assistance of an experienced trouble-shooter and advisor.

This screen print was produced with the photostencil method using a special positive transparency which can convert the continuous tones of a photograph or wash drawing into a distinct mass and texture effect. Regardless of the stencil technique employed, a "short" buttery ink consistency is generally recommended where it's important to retain maximum tonal and textural qualities of the artwork. Courtesy Martin J. Weber Co., New York.

When using manually operated equipment for printing large size editions, a two-man team expedites the operation, making it possible to produce several hundred impressions per hour. Shown here is the author with his assistant or "take-off" man. (Photo by Charles H. Coles.)

CHAPTER TWELVE

The printing procedure

After the rather lengthy discussion on ink formulation and color matching, you're by this time no doubt anxious to put your newly acquired knowledge to work on an actual printing project. Printing is the fun part of screen process technology, because you see the final results of your effort in black and white, or better still, in full color.

Basically, the printing procedure involves moving the squeegee from one side of the screen to the other—each movement producing a print. Moving that squeegee back and forth looks deceivingly simple; more so, if you watch an expert at work. Surprisingly, it takes a good deal of practice and dexterity to go about it smoothly and efficiently.

A Hypothetical Job

Let's take a hypothetical job, with the specifications noted below, and see how an experienced printer working with a "take-off" assistant handles it.

Art to be reproduced: A poster designed in three flat colors: background in lemon yellow with 1" white margin all around; design element and lettering in red and black.

Stock: 15" x 20" four-ply white cardboard.

Quantity: 250, plus a small number of "overs" for proofs and spoilage.

Stencils: Three; one for each color. All are handcut lacquer films.

Sequence of printings: First color—lemon yellow; second color—red; third color—black.

Type of ink: Quick drying oil based poster ink.

We'll assume that each stencil is prepared on a separate screen; inks matched, mixed, and pretested. The squeegee has been chosen with care, and register guides fastened in position. One master bed is used for all three screens; each screen fits the same set of hinges.

There are many important checkpoints which the printer would ordinarily be concerned with, both prior to and during the printing operation. We'll allude to these later on. At the moment we're pri-

marily interested in the setup and the actual printing procedure.

The stock is neatly placed on one side of the screen and drying racks are placed on the other side, so that there's an orderly flow of work from left to right.

Starting to print: To start with, the printer hooks up screen #1 (lemon-yellow). He places a card in the register guides, then lowers the screen. After stirring the ink mixture, to be sure that the ingredients are thoroughly interspersed, he pours a quantity of it into the masked-out area on the right side of the screen. He stands in front of the table, feet apart to assure good balance. Employing a one-hand squeegee, he places it in the screen, directly back of the ink mixture. Next firmly holding the grip handle of the squeegee with his right hand (while leaning over somewhat and resting the other hand on the screen frame), he then pushes a broad ribbon of ink smoothly across from one side of the screen to the other, going from right to left. In crossing, he maintains evenly distributed pressure throughout—his squeegee tilted slightly forward in the direction of the stroke. With the squeegee banked on the left side, he raises the screen, propping it up on its dropleg support. The first impression is made.

Normally, he would, at this juncture, run several impressions to be used as proof sheets and make whatever corrections might be required. We'll assume, at least for this hypothetical demonstration, that everything checks out, and that he's ready to go ahead with the edition printing.

Continuing the edition run: As soon as a card is printed, the take-off assistant places it on the rack for drying. The bed is cleared; the printer sets the next card in the guides and lowers the screen. For this stroke he holds the grip handle with his left hand (while resting the free hand on the screen frame). With the squeegee tilted forward in the direction of the stroke as before, he pushes the ink across—this time going from left to right.

Once more, he raises the screen. When the assistant takes the print off the bed, the printer positions the next card into the guides, lowers the screen, and pulls another impression. With each impression, he rhythmically shifts his position as he manipulates the squeegee, alternating between one hand and the other. He continues in this fashion until the last card of the edition is printed, pausing from time to time to inspect the print, and when necessary, replenish the ink supply. The entire run takes a little over an hour to complete, except for cleaning the screen, a job usually taken over by the assistant.

Cleaning up: The screen may be cleaned on the master bed, or disengaged from its hinges and transferred to a suitable table top or other flat surface. In the present instance, to save production time, the latter course is followed. While the assistant cleans the screen, the printer proceeds to set up for the red—screen #2.

Screen cleaning, the terminal step in the printing cycle, is an important aspect of maintenance. Unless this is done properly, the screen and squeegee may be ruined or impaired. As in the printing itself, it takes dexterity plus experience to do the job neatly and with dispatch.

The assistant prepares for cleaning by spreading several layers of newsprint paper under the screen. With a sharp-edged piece of stiff cardboard, he gathers and scoops up the leftover ink in the screen, and places it back in the container. In a similar manner, he removes whatever ink clings to the squeegee rubber. Then, with a plentiful supply of absorbent rags on hand, he proceeds to wash the screen using Varnolene—an effective, but inexpensive solvent of the mineral spirits type. Varnolene dries faster than kerosene and somewhat slower than turpentine. Swishing solvent-saturated rags over the entire surface, he applies the solvent not only to the open stencil area, but to all corners, periodically changing the layers of paper underneath. He cleans both sides of the screen as well as the frame, until not a vestige of ink is left. He follows up with a dry rag to mop up all traces of the solvent. The squeegee is cleaned with equal thoroughness. As a final measure, he examines screen and squeegee to make sure that they're scrupulously clean, completely free of ink or solvent. The entire cleaning operation from start to finish takes less than fifteen minutes.

In the meantime, the printer has completed his set-up for the second color. The screen is hooked into the master hinges on the bed, register guides checked, ink placed in the screen, squeegee selected, and so on. Because the poster inks selected for this job were of the quick-drying type, the early prints of the edition are now sufficiently dry and ready for the second printing.

The printing routine is the same for this, and the subsequent color. So is the cleaning procedure.

Now let's regard the printing demonstration retrospectively, focusing our attention on equipment, makeready, and production controls. All have a bearing on the efficacy of the printing operation and on the final printing results achieved.

The Screen Unit

Rigidity in frame construction is a prerequisite to control of register, particularly in multicolor printing. Corners must be well joined—reinforced with angle irons if necessary—to eliminate any possibility of twisting.

The fabric: The silk, or whatever fabric is stretched on the frame, must be taut; the tauter, the better. You can't get sharp printing or good register otherwise. A loosely stretched screen is likely to drag in the direction of the squeegee stroke. In so doing, it will not only blur the print, but shift the position of the image with each alternating motion of the squeegee. Mechanical silk stretchers are available, but they're expensive and can only be used with a limited number of frame sizes. Screen fabrics can be stretched very adequately by hand without the aid of mechanical contrivances. The only device needed is perhaps a pair of rubber-tipped grip pliers—the kind artists use for stretching canvas.

Dimensions of the screen: The size and proportion of the screen frame are important considerations, as well as the placement of the hinges. A screen constructed on a rectangular format and hinged to one of the long sides has an inherent operational advantage; it provides ample space for a supply of ink on both the right and left sides of the stencil image. In our hypothetical demonstration where the edition stock was 15″ x 20″, the inside measurements of the screen frame were 18″ x 30″. The 30″ length allowed for a bank of 5″ on either side for ink. A generous space allowance makes printing possible for longer periods of time, without having to stop too frequently to replenish the ink supply. Considerably less space is allowed top and bottom (just enough for the free movement of a full length squeegee). This keeps the ink from drifting into the open stencil area when the screen is in a raised position.

Working with a screen hinged on a long side enables the printer to take the most convenient position—center stage, that is, in front of the screen table. A front position offers the printer the best accessibility to the stock in feeding and take-off. At the same time this position permits him to squeegee from right-to-left and left-to-right—the accepted practice in the pictorial, poster, and general commercial field, when printing with manually-operated squeegee units. Automatic screen printing presses, however, many of which use square dimensioned screens, are designed to operate with an up-and-down, rather than side-to-side squeegee movement. This also holds true in the screening of textiles when the printing is done on long, open tables.

The printing bed: The printing bed has a lot to do with the quality of the finished print. Whereas under certain circumstances almost any kind of reasonably flat board can be put into service, professionals select their printing beds with utmost care to make sure that the surface is absolutely flat, smooth, and devoid of any evidence of configurations or warp. High spots on the bed show up as thin deposits of ink on the print; valleys appear as heavy deposits, especially when paper or other lightweight stock is used. Any surface irregularity will cause variations in depth of color, affect drying time, and quite frequently impede sharpness. It's good shop practice, whenever feasible, to cover the bed with a sheet of interchangeable, smooth cardboard. This protects it from ink and solvent smudges, and provides added assurance of evenness of the printing surface.

Many of the professional screen printing units, especially those designed for automatic squeegeeing, come equipped with a vacuum pump understructure and a bed, the surface of which has hundreds of tiny airholes. As the screen is lowered for the passing of the squeegee, the pump action is triggered, causing air to be sucked through the holes. This action holds the paper or other stock firmly in position during the printing. As the screen is raised (either manually or automatically) air suction stops, allowing the stock to be removed from the bed. Vacuum printing tables are generally employed in production runs on thin stock to keep the stock in a fixed position on the bed and prevent it from sticking to the underside of the screen mesh as the screen is raised. This not only assures better control of register, but sharper printing as well.

The Printing Table

For limited edition printing where production speed is of no particular consequence, the basic screen unit (consisting of screen hinged to a baseboard) can be set up almost anywhere. A sturdy pair of saw horses, a kitchen table, or for that matter, any available table-high surface can be used. For sustained printing on a commercial production basis, a well built table of proper height is a must.

A convenient table height for average size screens is 36", but that's variable. For extra large screens, a lower table permits better squeegee control and offers a better line of vision. The table surface may be level, or it may be sloped in the manner of an architectural drafting table. Some printers prefer working with a sloped table, because it helps balance the flow of ink when the screen is in a raised position during feeding and take-off.

A bottom shelf is an added convenience. It provides space for inks, solvents, wiping cloths, etc., and keeps them off the floor, yet within easy reach when needed. Two back posts incorporated in the table structure are useful for spring attachments, counterbalances, or other screen lifting devices.

Register Guides

Checking register guides constitutes another important aspect in the general preparation for printing. In large commercial shops this is usually the responsibility of the setup man or the shop foreman.

This manually operated "one-arm" screen printing unit has a perforated table top as well as a vacuum pump which provides suction that keeps the printing stock from lifting or shifting during the passing of the squeegee. Not only does this accelerate the speed of printing but also results in sharper impressions. Courtesy M & M Research Engineering Co., Butler, Wisconsin.

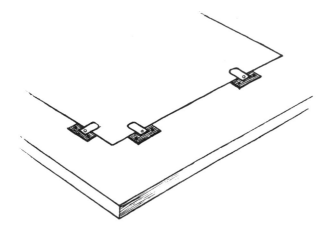

Clips over the register guides help keep paper and other flexible stock from shifting out of position.

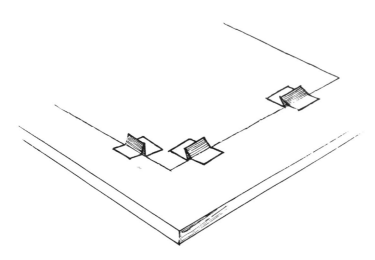

Foldover paper register guides are useful for limited edition printing of paper stock.

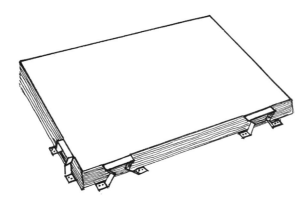

Collapsible, thin paperboard guides can be used for high stack feeding of paper stock where register is not a crucial factor.

The type of guides employed will depend on the nature and thickness of the stock and the number of copies to be printed. For example, heavy cardboard, glass, or wood panels require considerably thicker and more substantial guides than paper or thin cardboard. Similarly, extensive editions running into the thousands call for stronger and more durable guides than short editions. As a rule, it's best when the thickness of the guides matches the thickness of the stock being printed. Guides that are too thin may cause trouble in feeding; if they're appreciably higher than the stock, they may not only interfere with squeegee contact, but possibly damage the screen fabric as well.

In screen printing, as you already know, three register guides are used—one on the side, and two on the bottom. The guides are set carefully and fastened to the base flush against the bottom as well as on one of the side edges of the stock being printed. If the slightest bit askew, they'll contribute to faulty register. The side guide may be either on the right or left, to suit personal convenience. Whether the guide is on the right side or on the left side isn't important, as long as the same side is retained as the guide side throughout the printing of all colors of the job.

The sole function of the guides on the printing bed is to act as stops, fixing the position of the stock in relation to the screen image. Guides needn't be larger than 1½″ x ¾″, regardless of the size of the stock to be printed. They can be made of cardboard, fiberboard, acetate, or—for very short runs—of several layers of masking tape or gum paper. The most durable guides (those generally reserved for long runs or for printing on heavy stock) are lead slugs, the kind used as spacers in typesetting. These are available at all printers' supply houses, and come in an assortment of thicknesses.

For proper register control, guides must be firmly secured to the bed to eliminate the slightest possibility of jiggling or shifting in the course of the printing operation. They can be glued, cemented, stapled, or nailed down. As an additional measure in register control when printing on thin stock, small overhang clips can be attached to the guides to keep the stock from lifting away from the guides. The stock is fed into the guides as usual, but slipped under the overhang clips. The clips may be thin cardboard, metal, fiberboard, or acetate, extending about ¼″ onto the printing stock.

Once the guides are set, the experienced printer refrains from repositioning them. The only exception perhaps might come at the beginning of the run when the job is being proofed. Then slight adjustment might be necessary to bring the printed image into better register.

No matter how accurately the guides are set, or what other mechanical controls are provided to assure good register, the human element plays an important part in this phase of the printing procedure. Constant and unvarying care must be exercised in feeding the stock into the guides. The slightest irregularity will throw the register out of kilter, a condition that may show up dramatically in multicolor jobs.

For "rush" jobs, when printing on thin paper stock in sizable quantities, it's sometimes feasible to use a high-feed, collapsible fiberboard guide. A stack of ten or more papers, well jogged, can be set into the guides at one time. As the height diminishes with each succeeding print, the guides lower automatically to the level of the top sheet. Printing with collapsible guides is expedient only when extreme accuracy of register isn't a crucial factor in the quality of the print.

The Squeegee

Squeegees can be cut to any size, but hardly anyone would think of cutting down a long squeegee just because he requires a shorter one for the job on hand. Most commercial screen shops have an assortment of squeegees in a wide range of sizes. The size of the squeegee selected for the job is determined by the smaller dimension of the screen. For that 15″ x 20″ demonstration project, the inside measurements of the screen were 18″ x 30″. A 16″ squeegee was used, a size which allowed for a 1″ play, top and bottom. If the squeegee had been appreciably smaller, say 9″ or 10″, it still would have been possible to use it, but would have required two strokes to cover the same area. This would not only be time consuming, but would most likely leave an objectionable streak where the two crossings overlapped.

The squeegee selected may be the kind that's gripped with one hand, or with two. It's largely a matter of personal preference and what you get accustomed to. Artists and students, for the most part, find the two-hand squeegee easier to manipulate, whereas commercial printers are more partial to the one-hand squeegee mainly because it permits faster production.

With the one-hand squeegee (which the printer used in the demonstration), the printing is done by pushing the squeegee with the right and left hand alternately, each stroke producing a separate impression. This procedure calls for a certain degree of ambidexterity since equal pressure must be exerted alternately with each hand. With the two-hand squeegee, both hands are used simultaneously, the pressure distributed between both hands.

In printing with a two-hand squeegee, the printer takes the usual position in front of the screen unit. To make a right-to-left stroke, the right hand is at the near end of the squeegee; the left hand is at the far end. To make a left-to-right stroke, the position of the hands is reversed; the right hand is at the far end, the left hand is at the near end.

Another distinguishing difference in the manipulation of the two types of squeegees is this: a two-hand squeegee is *pulled* across the screen as the operator takes a position in *front* of the squeegee; whereas a one-hand squeegee is *pushed* across, as the operator takes a position in *back* of the squeegee.

Regardless of the type of squeegee used, it should be held at a forward angle (about 65°), tipped in the direction of the stroke. To counteract a natural tendency to straighten the squeegee as the end of the stroke is approached, it helps to sway the upper part of the body following the movement of the squeegee, and to stand with feet apart to maintain a balanced position. For best printing results, whatever pressure is applied must be evenly distributed throughout the crossing. Sluggish or uneven pressure yields prints lacking in sharpness and uniformity. A good, clean sweep of the squeegee leaves a minimum of ink in its wake, with no evidence of ripples or puddles. One crossing of the squeegee in most cases is sufficient. A second crossing increases the consumption of ink and slows up the printing operation. However, where an unusually thick deposit of ink is desired, either for greater opacity, better penetration, or whatever, a "flood" or a multiple stroke may be expeditious.

It isn't necessary—nor desirable—to transport the entire supply of ink in the screen with every crossing of the squeegee. Only a limited amount need be picked up—not much more than is required to make the impression, with enough ink left over for the return stroke.

It's the quality and the condition of the rubber (not the shape of the casing, or whether the squeegee has or lacks a grip handle) that determine the working efficiency of the squeegee. The best squeegee rubber is made of neoprene, koroseal, plasticol, or other synthetic materials possessing extraordinary durability. They hold a sharper edge for a longer period of time than natural rubber, are free from warpage, and are impervious to all solvents and inks used in screen printing. They cost more than natural rubber, but since a squeegee lasts practically forever, the cost differential isn't significant.

A good grade of rubber keeps its true edge for thousands of impressions. Whenever it does require a bit of sharpening, a dozen or so strokes over a garnet or sandpaper board will restore it to its original state.

We said before, the squeegee lasts practically forever. That's true only if it's properly cared for. This is an important part of shop maintenance. The squeegee must be cleaned thoroughly after use. No trace of ink must remain. Crusted, dried-up ink shortens the life of the rubber, robbing it of its natural resilience and flexibility.

In passing, it's interesting to note that though a squeegee with a sharp-edged blade is a standard requirement for general printmaking purposes, there are occasions when a rounded or a wedge-shaped blade may be more functionally desirable. A rounded blade is used when a heavier deposit of ink is desired; a wedge-shaped blade sometimes works out

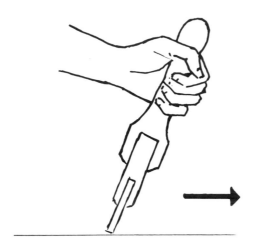

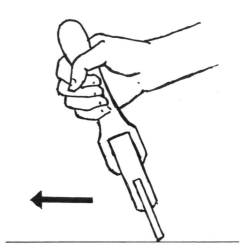

Shown here is the hand grip of a one-hand squeegee in crossing the screen, going from left to right.

Shown here is the hand grip of a one-hand squeegee in crossing the screen, going from right to left.

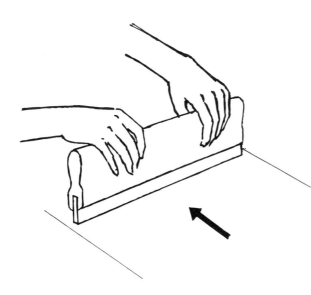

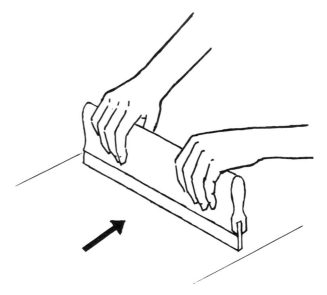

Shown here is the hand grip of a two-hand squeegee in crossing the screen, going from right to left.

Shown here is the hand grip of a two-hand squeegee in crossing the screen, going from left to right.

better where penetration is an important factor, as when printing on certain types of fabric.

For printing on jumbo-size screens, requiring the use of extra long squeegees, two operators work together as a team. They stand opposite each other across the table, each bearing down on his end of the squeegee, as they coordinate their efforts in pushing it from one side of the screen to the other.

Proofing and Makeready

The run isn't ready for full-scale production until proofs are pulled and carefully checked. It may be necessary to make minor adjustments in the guides, or touch up pinholes or leaks which have up until now gone undetected in the preparation of the stencil. The ink, too, may require modifications in color match, degree of opacity, or working consistency, although presumably these have been previously checked out.

Proofs sometimes show a consistent blur which is attributable to a drag in the screen fabric as the squeegee is pushed across it. Adjustments in the makeready for what is called "off-contact" printing may then be necessary. This is accomplished by slightly propping up the screen frame either front or back. Also folded pieces of gum paper may be attached to the underside of the screen to serve as breakers. In this way the mesh will snap away from the print immediately after the edge of the squeegee blade passes over it. Off-contact printing generally yields sharper printing results, and many of the automatic screen presses are engineered with that principle in mind.

Initial proofing is usually done on white newsprint or other inexpensive paper to conserve stock. Newsprint makes an ideal proofing material: its white color permits true color evaluation. It offers an absorbent, receptive surface for the ink. Newsprint is available in a number of convenient sizes both in sheets and rolls.

The usual procedure in pulling proofs is to start with newsprint first until the impression comes through sharp and clear. This is followed with several clean proofs on the edition stock for a final okay. In multicolor work, the proofs on the edition stock are set aside as "master" sheets to be used for all subsequent colors in the sequence of printings.

Once the proofing is completed and the edition printing is on the way, the printer doesn't blithely assume that the entire run will unerringly match the quality of the master prints. From time to time he checks for pinholes, blurs, misregister, or other irregularities which may develop as the printing progresses.

A certain amount of spoilage of stock is inevitable during proofing and printing. On a commercial basis, two or three percent for each color printed is considered average. Understandably, the percentage will vary with the nature of the job being printed, the extent of the edition, and the number of colors in-

This cross section schematic view of "off-contact" printing shows the momentary point of contact between the screen fabric and the printing surface, and the immediate lift away of the fabric.

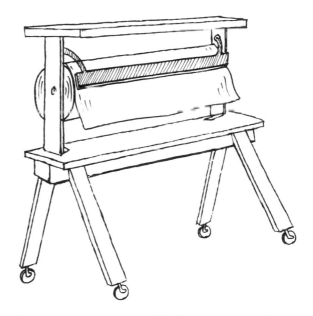

A roll of newsprint paper with dispenser mounted on a movable saw horse will come in handy in any print workshop for pre-production proofing and washups.

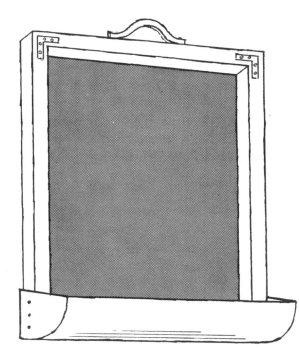

A screen frame, suitable for printing directly onto walls or other upright surfaces, has a trough on the bottom that holds the ink supply.

Here's a makeready for printing on high stock and three dimensional surfaces such as books, toys, boxes, etc.

This simple mechanical jig prints directly on bottles, tumblers, and other round-surfaced objects. Courtesy Atlas Silk Screen Supply Co., Chicago, Illinois.

Semi-automatic and completely automatic screen printing presses are available in a wide range of sizes and models to accommodate specific production requirements. Shown here is a small size unit capable of screening over 1,000 impressions per hour. Courtesy M & M Research Engineering Co., Butler, Wisconsin.

volved. In starting out, a sufficient number of sheets must be set aside for possible spoilage. This avoids the predicament of running short of the required amount of stock needed to fill the order.

Printing on High Stock and Three Dimensional Objects

Up to this point we've been talking about printing on paper, thin cardboard, and the like. For flat stock, not more than ¼", there's no radical departure either in the setup or in the printing procedure. The only difference is that screen hinges may have to be shimmed up a bit with several pieces of cardboard, and the register guides increased in height to accommodate the thickness of the stock.

In handling much thicker stock—for example, heavy plywood, boxes, bound books, and similar flat-surfaced objects—special jigs can be easily improvised to enable the screen to come down level with the surface being printed. Some such arrangement is shown.

You'll note that wood blocks matching the thickness of the stock to be printed are fastened to the bed. These do double duty: they provide a raised platform for supporting the screen frame and, at the same time, serve as points of register.

The screen frame, as you can see, is not fastened to the bed itself, but rather, to a back bar to raise it to the level of the stock.

With this simple arrangement, any flat surface can be screened, regardless of the nature of the stock or its thickness.

The principle of printing through a screen stencil is basically the same for cylindrical as for flat surfaces. The setup and procedure, however, by which the printed image is applied to the surface differ radically. In printing on a flat surface, the stock is placed in position on the bed. Upon lowering the screen, an impression is produced by pushing the squeegee across from one side to the other. In printing on a cylindrical surface, the object is positioned, not on a bed, but on a set of ball-bearing rollers located on a special chassis below the screen. To make a print, the screen is lowered close to, but not actually in direct contact with, the object below. The squeegee, fixed to the screen frame, remains stationary; it's the screen, not the squeegee,

that's moved from side to side on a track. As the screen moves in one direction, the momentary pressure of the squeegee bearing down on the screen contacts the object below and causes it to rotate on its rollers in the opposite direction. The object receives the printed image as it rotates under the screen.

Homemade jigs can be improvised for screening directly on cylindrical objects such as bottles and tumblers. However, commercial units specificially designed for the purpose are easily available. They involve little expenditure, are versatile, and simple to operate. The unit shown here is typical of a number of similar, manually-operated round surface printers. These are primarily intended for limited-scale production with an output of thirty to 150 impressions per hour. The rate of printing depends largely on the circumference of the object and its weight—and the availability of a capable take-off assistant to lend a hand in the operation.

The more sophisticated equipment designed for mass production is power driven, and is adaptable for screening a wide variety of round, oval, or conical objects at speeds in excess of 3,000 impressions per hour. The equipment includes coordinated high temperature ovens which not only hasten the drying process, but permanently fuse the ink to the surface on which it is applied.

Printing with Automated Equipment

Rapid strides made in automation have escalated screen printing from a handcraft to a mass production process which approaches the speed of letterpress, offset, and related graphic arts. Completely automatic screen printing presses are being developed for production speeds of 5,000 impressions or more per hour. Accompanying these technological advances in printing presses are developments in coordinated drying facilities that are geared to keep pace with stepped-up production.

Of course this equipment is all a long way from the basic screen printing equipment you started out with. You'll find, however, that the simple screen and squeegee unit, with minor modifications, will be adequate for most printing projects that you're likely to undertake in your early experience with the process.

CHAPTER THIRTEEN

Screen printing on fabrics

Screen printing on fabrics, the way it's done in large textile printing plants, calls for the investment of thousands of dollars for specially constructed screen tables, curing ovens, and other elaborate installations. Very creditable results, however, are achievable on a limited edition basis with conventional screen units. Modified setups that can be put together at nominal cost also produce good results. In this chapter we'll concern ourselves mainly with equipment and procedures adaptable for the home, classroom, and studio workshop.

There are two basic approaches to screening on fabrics. In one, the fabric (as continuous lengths or piece goods) is pinned or otherwise fastened to a long, open table, and printed with a portable screen that's moved from one position to the next. In the other, the fabric is positioned on the bed of a hinged screen unit, and printed in a manner not unlike paper or cardboard stock. Bear this distinction in mind: when printing on an *open table,* the screen is brought to the fabric; when printing with a *hinged screen,* the fabric is brought to the screen.

The Open Table Method

The major piece of special equipment required for the open table method is a flat surfaced table. Its size is determined by the size of the fabric you plan to work with and by the floor space available. The table need not be much larger than an ironing board, or it may approach the dimensions of the huge tables employed in industry—some measuring more than 6' across, long enough to roll out a 60-yard bolt of material.

Before venturing into production involving equipment and techniques for printing extensive yardage, it's advisable first to gain experience with piece goods and yardage of limited lengths. Some of the country's leading designers, who have attained eminence in the field of screen printed fabrics, are professionally identified with custom-made designs produced on a limited production basis, with simple equipment set up in home studios and in modest-sized workshops.

If, and when, you should decide to pursue a professional career in the design and production of screen printed fabrics, you can determine, at that time, what course of action to follow—limited or full-scale production, whether piece goods or continuous bolt printing—with equipment to match the scope and extent of your production plans.

The Printing Table

Here are some notes on the basic construction, the surface padding, and the register guide rail.

Basic construction: You have a choice of a permanent, rigidly constructed table, or one which is nothing more than a flat board that can be placed on saw horses when in use, dismantled, and stored away when not needed.

The functional part of the table is the printing surface, or top board. In this regard, there are no standard specifications to follow either in the matter of size, thickness, or type of wood used. Generally speaking, the larger the board, the thicker and more rigid it must be to maintain sufficient flatness. For a 4' x 12' surface, the board might well be ¾" or more in thickness. A thinner board could be put into service if the underside is properly reinforced with wood or metal cleats. As to composition, the board may be maple, pine, a good grade of chipboard, heavy plywood, Formica, steel plate, or any other material least subject to warpage or configurations.

You may eventually want to avail yourself of a printing table that's professionally constructed—one purchased ready-made or built to your exact specifications. In the meantime, a home-built table, any solid board, or even a flat closet door placed on a support, at a height 32"–35" from the floor, could serve your purpose just as well. The top surface may be level or tilted at the back end, but this is largely a matter of personal choice and convenience.

Surface padding: Regardless of the particular dimensions of the table top, its thickness, composition, or height from the floor, it's important for the surface to be absolutely flat throughout. This is a fundamental requirement that allows for no compromise.

Padding the surface will help to counteract any trace of unevenness in the board. If the table is unvaryingly flat to begin with, padding takes on relatively less importance as a surface leveler, but offers other distinct advantages. In addition to serving as a protective covering for the table, it provides a receptive surface for pinning the fabric. It also acts as a cushion to permit better color penetration when that's an important element in the quality of the finished print.

The padding may be prepared any number of ways. In the trade they generally use a layer of ¼″ felt or sponge rubber covered with cotton or canvas cloth. This in turn is protected with a vinyl or oilcloth sheeting; on top of this sheeting is stretched an interchangeable coverall of expendable muslin. In some instances, a roll of newsprint or kraft paper is used as an expedient substitute for the muslin.

Don't assume from the foregoing that padding is an inflexible requirement. Sometimes, a hard, unyielding surface is preferable. It all depends on the nature of the fabric, consistency of the printing medium, and the final outcome desired. The conditions that call for surface padding are best determined by professional judgment based on experience.

If you plan to use a portable board rather than a fixed table top, it's a good idea to make it reversible; one side can be padded and resilient, the other, unpadded and hard. That way, you can use either side, whichever is best for the job at hand.

Register guide rail: The most efficient system yet devised for control of register uses a guide rail, against which the screen is placed in predetermined positions. On an amateur level, the guide rail may be merely a length of firring strip with protruding nails or pegs serving as register stops. However, it may be dispensed with entirely, and the screen visually positioned over a grid penciled in on the cloth.

For precision register, the guide rail is usually a length of ³⁄₁₆″ gauge, 2″ x 2″ angle iron. This is permanently secured to the surface of the table, close to the edge of one of the long sides, and running parallel to it. The guide rail serves a dual function: (a) as an elongated stanchion for lining up the screen frame, thus controlling the vertical (up-and-down) register; and (b) as a carrier for a series of movable clamps which control the horizontal (side-to-side) register. The clamps, or "stops" as they are called, are small metal cylinders machine-tooled with a cut groove to fit over the rail. By a turn of a set screw, the stops can be locked to fixed positions on the rail, corresponding to the measured-off distances between design repeats. Thus, at any one time, the rail may have two, three, or as many as fifty or more stops, depending on the number of times the screen has to be moved to complete the entire printing sequence.

The Screen Frame

The frame is constructed in the same manner as the standard-type frame used for poster printing, except

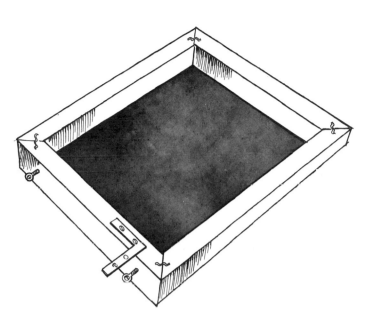

For controlling the register when screening textiles with the open table method, screen frames with screw-eyes and angle iron attachments are generally used.

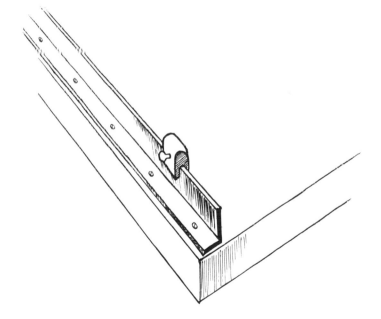

This view shows a register stop clamped in position to a guide rail for textile screening with the open table method.

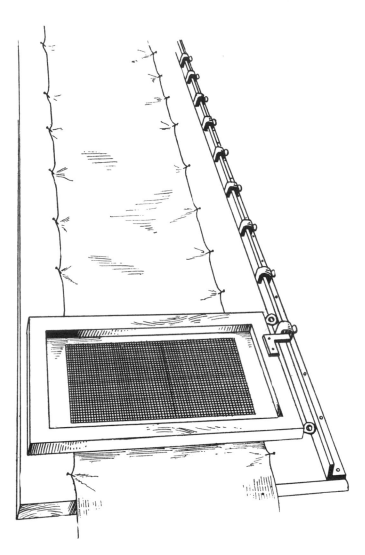

This overhead view of an open screen printing table shows a screen frame registered against one of the stops clamped to the guide rail.

that it's made of lighter weight lumber since it's carried manually. As to dimensions, the frame is somewhat square in proportion; it's normally 10″ or 12″ longer than the width of the material being printed.

The screen frame for the open table method doesn't have hinges. Instead, it's equipped with several simple fittings to coordinate with the guide rail and register stops on the printing table. The fittings consist of an L-shaped angle iron (about 3″ x 3″) and two small screw eyes. The angle iron is attached to the top of the frame facing the guide rail. It may be placed toward the right or left side—it doesn't matter as long as one arm is secured to the frame, the other protruding outward. The part that protrudes rides above the rail, and serves as an extending arm for contacting each stop, as the frame is moved from one position on the rail to the next. The screw eyes are set into the back edge of the screen frame to face the rail, and are spaced as far apart as possible.

In the printing position, the screen frame doesn't touch the rail directly. The two screw eyes serve as bumpers or points of contact between rail and frame. By a turn or two of one or both screw eyes, the frame can be moved close to, or further away from the rail, either in a parallel or slightly angular position. The screw eyes serve an additional purpose. They provide a smooth metal to metal alignment between frame and rail, minimizing the effects of any warp on the guide side of the frame.

The screen frame (with extending arm and screw eyes set in place) when lined up with the guide rail on the printing table is shown here.

The Printing Procedure

When printing with the open table method, whether on continuous yardage or piece goods, the fabric must be kept from shifting as the screen is positioned over it and the squeegee moved across. In single color printing, where patterns are neither adjacent nor interlocking, a slight shift may not be too serious and hardly discernible in the finished print. In multicolor work, particularly where tight register control is a major production requirement, even an imperceptible shift in the fabric can show up glaringly, and mar an otherwise perfect job.

The fabric may be held in place by an adhesive compound or by pins. The adhesive compound used dries with a surface which remains tacky for an extended period of time. When material is pressed against this surface, it's held in position; yet the material releases easily without resistance and without marring the underside. For pinning, ordinary straight pins may be employed, or better still, the T-headed kind which are easy to insert and pull out. Staples may also be used. When working with heavy bodied material such as canvas or drill cloth, some printers roll the bolt of fabric across the table and keep it tautly stretched with the aid of a ratchet device at both ends.

Various register jigs can be improvised when using a small size screen for repeat designs when production is confined to limited output. Courtesy The American Crayon Co., New Jersey.

In the printing procedure, the screen is set down on the fabric in planned sequential positions, controlled by the register stops on the guide rail. The print is made with an up-and-down stroke, i.e., by pushing the squeegee away from the operator and back again. Usually a two-hand squeegee is used. For most fabrics, one up-and-down stroke is sufficient. For monk's cloth, felt, toweling, and other rough-textured material, several squeegee crossings are frequently required to produce better ink penetration.

If the screen is small, the job can easily be handled by one person. For large-size screens, it's customary to have two people work as a team facing each other across the table; one holds the screen in position while the other operates the squeegee. Sometimes they operate the squeegee together. After each impression, the screen is carefully lifted and set into the next position and the printing routine continued.

When printing piece goods, if the individual units are laid out with ample space separating one from the other, the printing can be done in unbroken sequence. Where the individual units are closely spaced, or when handling continuous yardage with connecting patterns, the work must be planned so that the printing is done in alternate or print and skip sequence. This avoids the possibility of smudging caused by setting down the screen on the wet print. The first sequence of printings may start out at even numbered stops and upon reaching the end of the table, the second sequence can begin, this time at odd numbered stops. This print and skip procedure is followed throughout the run.

In commercial textile printing, where extra long tables are used—and with a battery of fans, or other facilities to accelerate drying—the ink is sufficiently dry on the early prints, long before the end of the table is reached. This enables a follow-up crew to start the second sequence.

The Hinged Screen Method

The standard hinged screen and bed unit used for printing on paper, cardboard, and other flat surfaces is adaptable for printing on fabrics, whether piece goods or extended yardage.

Piece Goods Printing

When the material that is to be screen printed is in small units, the routine printing procedure is followed: the material is placed in the register guides on the bed, the screen lowered, the impression pulled, the screen raised, and the wet print set aside for drying. This presupposes that there's sufficient body and weight to the material (as in the case of pyroxylin-coated cloth, felt, and heavy cotton) to permit it being registered in the same manner as paper or cardboard. However, it's often difficult to position highly flexible material such as unbacked satin, silk, jersey, and similar soft goods, or material which is unselvaged or unevenly cut. Conventional guides don't work out too well, especially where close register multicolor printing is involved.

One way of assuring accurate register control when handling such material is to mount each piece on uniform-size newsboard or other low cost board. In printing, the material can then be registered in the normal fashion. Another way is to use a flap guide device which permits a visual rather than a mechanical register.

Mounting on board: The material to be printed can be mounted in any of a number of ways: it can be stapled, taped, or attached with a temporary textile adhesive formulated for just that purpose. The adhesive can be applied to the board by screen, brush, or scraper—whichever is most expedient. When mounted, difficult to register material can be fed into fixed guides, just like ordinary cardboard or other rigid stock. After printing (in one, or as many colors as required) the material is stripped off and the boards set aside for re-use in the future.

Flap guide register: With the flap guide setup, the following procedure can be used effectively. A sheet of thin acetate (or other transparent tissue large enough to cover the area of the design image) is stapled or taped at one edge to the surface of the bed. It's attached so that it folds over like a page in a book. While in a down position, a master impression is printed on the acetate and allowed to dry.

To register the material, it's placed on the bed and the acetate flapped over it. The material is then visually jockeyed into position to line up with the master impression. The acetate is folded back out of the way, permitting the material to be printed. This procedure is repeated for the entire run. By employing a flap guide device, any material can be printed in register, regardless of its shape, cut, or degree of flexibility.

Yardage Printing

For printing long strips of cloth or other flexible material in one section and as one operation, an extra large screen and bed unit can be constructed to accommodate the job on hand. Many advertising banners—some measuring fifteen feet in length—are commercially produced in this manner. However, where the expense involved in building an oversized screen and bed unit isn't warranted (or where floor space doesn't permit it), it's possible to use ordinary size screens for extended lengths, or even for material in bolt form. This is done by shifting the material on the bed in measured out distances, and printing it in sequential or alternate repeats. Register is controlled with the aid of a flap guide. As the printed material comes off the bed, it's hung up for drying by draping it festoon-fashion on sticks laid across a scaffolding of two long parallel bars. The higher the bars are from the floor, the longer the folds may be, and consequently the less floor space will be required.

When printing from the bolt, the setup may include two rotating axles. One is rigged up at the feeding end of the bed and holds the bolt of cloth; the other is situated at the far end of the festoon drying structure and serves as the core for rolling up the cloth as it dries.

Stencil Techniques for Screening on Fabrics

Practically any of the standard stencil techniques may be employed for textile printing: tusche (or other resist), blockout, handcut film, or photographic methods. The choice depends on the type of ink used, the extent of the edition, and in large measure on the nature of the design. A finely detailed and carefully rendered pattern would readily suggest itself to photostencils while a more extemporaneous art treatment might lend itself more to one of the resist type of stencils. Quite a number of fabric designers who do their own printing favor tusche or latex resists. A wax resist is preferred by others. The wax resist method not only eliminates the need for washing out with solvents, but is, according to some, an easier medium to work with than either tusche or latex. In industry, where stencils often have to last for thousands of yards and innumerable re-runs, the direct photostencil method is used extensively.

All stencils, no matter how they're produced, can be fortified with a hard-drying, caustic resist enamel, polyurethane, or varnish. This is done by coating the entire top surface of the screen with the fortifier. Then a solvent-damp cloth is immediately applied to the *underside* of the screen to remove whatever fortifier is lodged in the open (printing) parts of the stencil. When bone dry, the underside of the screen is similarly coated, this time rubbing the solvent-damp cloth over the *top* surface. A stencil produced in this manner possesses maximum durability, since it's virtually locked in between two impregnable coatings.

The screen fabric may be silk, nylon, or dacron the same as for poster printing. In the commercial textile field, however, multifilament dacron is generally favored as a screen fabric because of its superior tensile strength, excellent penetration, and dimensional stability. It's also comparatively less expensive.

Textile Inks

No special ink formulations would be needed for screen printing on fabrics, were it not for the fact that inks normally used on paper and cardboard are likely to bleach or wash out with repeated launderings and dry cleaning. Furthermore, standard inks applied to cloth have a tendency to crock (rub off) and to stiffen the surface after drying. These characteristics do not impose too serious a limitation when printing on nonwearable material such as wall

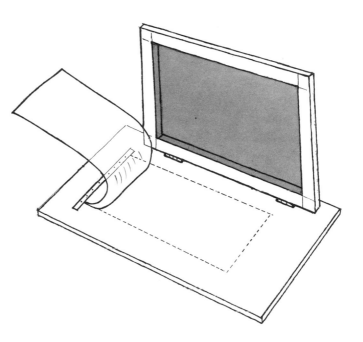

A flap guide device with transparent overlay such as this allows any material, regardless of its shape or flexibility, to be printed in exact register.

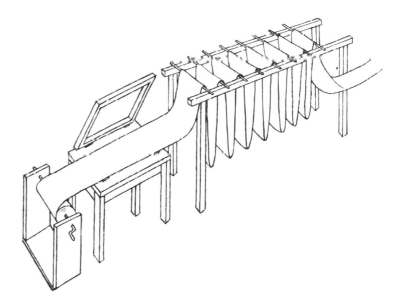

Festoon-type drying is practical when using a hinged screen for printing on cloth, vinyl, wallpaper, and other continuous yardage surfaces.

hangings, cloth signs, advertising novelties, and the like. For dress fabrics, however, and scarves, tablecloths, towels, T-shirts, and similar washable soft goods, it's important for the printed fabric to be colorfast, and retain its original flexibility. To date, there's no ink or dyestuff made that unequivocally satisfies these prerequisites without the additional step of a *curing* or a *fixing* process. Even the best of dyestuffs, imported from Germany and Switzerland, require postprint treatment.

Ink technology in the textile field represents a highly sophisticated area of research and continuing experimentation involving a prodigious variety of organic and synthetic formulations. A good many of these formulations have been developed during the course of years by company-employed chemists and color experts for the exclusive use of major textile printing firms. As time goes on, however, an increasing number of textile inks are being made commercially available. These, for all practical purposes, approach the best of ink formulations that previously had been in the private domain. The fabric printer today has a wide choice of ready to use inks available to him, as well as compatible ingredients that can easily be combined to suit his special needs.

Mainly, textile inks can be classified into three major groups: oleoresinous paints and lacquers, dyestuffs, and emulsion-type inks.

Oleoresinous paints and lacquers: These come in a full spectrum of bright, ready to use colors and are specially formulated to contain low crock agents. There are several kinds, both in paint and lacquer form. Those that dry mainly by oxidation are opaque, making it possible to print a light color on a dark ground, and on a variety of fabrics—awning material, game cloths, T-shirt material, upholstery, and slipcover material. Colors dry with a fair degree of flexibility. The range of normal drying time is extensive—from three hours to as much as twenty-four, depending largely on the nature of the material and the particular formulation of the ink.

The line of inks that dry by evaporation are for the most part transparent, and are intended primarily for unsized, white or light colored fabrics. Overlapping colors planned in proper sequence produce multiple color effects with a minimum of printings. Flexibility is good, but is improved by postprint heat treatment. Normal drying time is twenty to forty minutes.

Dyestuffs: Whereas oleoresinous paints and lacquers affect the hand (i.e., the softness or flexibility after drying) of the cloth to a greater or lesser extent, dyes don't—or do so only minimally. Pigment particles in paints and lacquers when applied to cloth via the vehicle rest on the surface or at best surround the fibers of the cloth. With dyes, on the other hand, the pigment particles in solution are integrated in the cloth. Upon postprint treatment (steaming and washing) these particles chemically bond with the fibers, resulting in maximum flexibility and color permanence.

There are many types of dye formulations: direct dyes, vat dyes, acid dyes, basic dyes, reactive dyes, etc. In the family of dye compounds, vat dyes have unexcelled fastness to light and washing, and therefore are used extensively in commercial textile printing. Because of their high index of acidity, vat dyes require exceptionally durable stencils, especially if they're intended for long runs.

Simplified dye preparations in paste form are now available which are easy for the beginner to use. They can be printed with any type of water resistant stencil. All colors are brilliant, intermixable, and will withstand repeated launderings and dry cleaning. Postprint treatment of dyes on an extensive commercial scale is a highly complex procedure involving special equipment. However, the beginner can get very acceptable results by setting his dyes with a hot iron, or exposing the fabric to strong sunlight or ultraviolet rays.

The colors can be used directly from the container without the addition of thinners or reducers. Being water-soluble, no other solvent but water is necessary for cleaning screen and squeegee. The best results are obtained with white or light colored fabrics which are free from starch or other sizing.

Emulsion-type inks: Newly developed emulsion-type inks are rapidly gaining in popularity as the choice medium for limited edition textile printing and to a certain extent for full-scale production as well. Emulsion inks print smoothly and easily. They dry fairly quickly, are economical to use, and are suitable for printing a wide assortment of fabrics including sheers, crepes, satins, percales, and flannels. Colors may be combined with one another in any proportion to produce compound shades. When properly printed and cured, emulsion-type inks don't affect the hand of most fabrics. It's for this reason that they're especially applicable for dress goods, tablecloths, scarves, curtain and drapery material.

Emulsion-type inks are obtainable either as premixed pastes in an assortment of distinct colors, or as clear emulsions designed to be intermixed with pigment concentrates. The latter type permits greater choice in color selection. The emulsion itself is comparatively inexpensive, and doesn't spoil if kept in a closed container. Where very large quantities are required on a continuing basis, the emulsion can be readily made up in the shop with simple ingredients supplied by the manufacturer.

Pigment concentrates come in a full array of brilliant colors with exceptionally high tinting power. In use, one part of pigment concentrate is added to ten to twenty parts of emulsion; the ratio varies with the

(Right) "Seaweed", the pattern shown, is the type of all-over textile pattern screened effectively with easy-to-use, colorfast, water-based emulsion inks. Courtesy the Prang Textile Studio of The American Crayon Co., New Jersey.

chromatic intensity desired. The combining of pigment concentrates and emulsion is usually done with a high-speed mixer or homogenizer.

Until quite recently, emulsion-type inks had been unalterably transparent which restricted their use to white or light colored fabrics. This limitation has largely been removed with the introduction of a newly perfected white pigment base. When added to the color mixtures, this base makes them sufficiently opaque so that light colors can be printed on a dark fabric with a fair degree of success.

Emulsion-type inks can be formulated to print as an oil based or water based medium, depending upon the composition of the emulsion. Artists, students, and limited edition printers find it more congenial to work with the water based type. It has no objectionable odor, isn't flammable, and doesn't need cleaning solvents since screens and squeegees can be washed with water.

Treatment of the fabric after printing usually consists of drying and curing. Drying is carried out by merely hanging the fabric and letting the air get at it for as long a period as feasible; the longer the better. Proper curing is essential in order to polymerize the resins used as binders for the pigment, thereby assuring maximum fastness. Curing for five minutes at 280°–300° F. is recommended for most fabrics. However, factors of time and temperature are influenced to some extent by the type of fabric and the type of heat used.

For the final outcome it's important that the fabric be free from starch or any other sizing before it's printed. If the fabric contains sizing it will seriously impede the curing process. It's therefore desirable that sized fabrics be prewashed before printing. This holds true not only when printing with emulsion-type inks but with any type of textile ink where flexibility and color fastness are important.

A final word: Regardless of the type of ink you use, follow the example set by all printers of textiles. Prior to printing the edition, pull several strike sheets on the actual fabric. Test for compatibility of ink to fabric, flexibility and color fastness. These and other factors will be relevant to the final outcome of the finished print.

CHAPTER FOURTEEN

What do you do if...

In spite of the inherent simplicity of screen printing, both in principle and practice, many technical problems are likely to arise. These can be a source of frustration, especially if the cause is unknown. This chapter presents a diagnostic review of some of the most prevalent of these problems, with helpful suggestions for solving them—or better still, averting them in the future by identifying their cause.

Equipment and Makeready

Problem 1: *The hinges that hold the screen to the printing bed get wobbly after a while, resulting in a side-to-side movement of the screen.*

Possible Cause A—The screws used to attach the hinges were either too short to begin with, or have loosened up.

Suggested Remedy—If tightening the screws doesn't help, replace them with longer ones.

Possible Cause B—The hinge pins are worn.

Suggested Remedy—Either replace them with new ones, or bend them a bit so that they will make a tighter fit. You can also do this: with the screen lowered, nail two wood cleats to the bed, one snugly at each side of the screen frame.

Problem 2: *There's something wrong with the gum paper binding on the screen. It doesn't seem to hold.*

Possible Cause—The chances are there's nothing wrong with the gum paper, but with the way it's been applied.

Suggested Remedy—It's important that the surface, to which the gum paper is applied, be free of any evidence of dust or grease. When wetting the gum paper, be sure to leave no dry spots. Strips of gum paper may be dipped in a tray of water, or moistened with a sponge. If a sponge is used, pass it across the gummed surface once or twice. No more. Repeated passings with the wet sponge remove the glue, rather than moisten it. After the gum paper is adhered, rub it down with a dry cloth.

Problem 3: *A rip develops in the silk during printing.*

Possible Cause—A pin, tack, or other sharp, pointed object may have found its way into the ink mixture, or onto the printing surface.

Suggested Remedy — Remove the object which caused the damage. Then carefully clean the area surrounding the rip. A rip that develops outside of the printing area can often be repaired with a carefully applied patch. To do this, saturate two pieces of thin paper (cut a little larger than the rip) with quick drying lacquer, placing one on the top surface of the rip, the other directly underneath it. The lacquer serves both as an adhesive and as a protective coat. The patch, if applied well, is permanent. It will not impair the use of the screen. In future jobs, however, the position of the design image will be restricted.

If the rip occurs within the printing area, there's little that can be done about repairing it while in the printing stage. With cautious handling, however, printing can often be continued without the quality of the print being seriously affected. After the edition is finished and the screen reclaimed, the rip can be patched as described.

Problem 4: *When the screen is lifted, the squeegee has a tendency to topple over and drop out of the screen.*

Possible Cause—The screen is raised too high.

Suggested Remedy—Don't raise the screen higher than is necessary for inserting and removing the printing stock. It also helps to prop up the far end of the printing bed about 5" or 6", thereby reducing the angle of the screen in its raised position.

Problem 5: *The squeegee in the screen doesn't seem to have enough traction to stay put; every so often it slides into the ink mixture and "falls on its face."*

Possible Cause—The screen takes on a slippery surface because of certain lubricating properties in the ink.

Suggested Remedy—Attach a small strip of wood or plastic to the top of the squeegee casing to act as a buffer. Another suggestion is to wedge a length of nail or rod into each end of the squeegee casing at a height considerably above the screen frame. This overhanging extension will keep the squeegee from falling into the ink.

Problem 6: *When stretching the screen fabric to the frame, tension rips often develop at points where the tacks are placed.*

Possible Cause A—The tacks aren't hammered down deeply enough. It's the head of the tack, not the shaft, that anchors the fabric to the frame.

Suggested Remedy—Hammer the tacks all the way down, so that the flat disks of the heads rest firmly on the fabric.

Possible Cause B—The tacks are spaced too far apart to withstand the pull of the screen fabric.

Suggested Remedy—Space the tacks an inch or less from each other; the closer the better. You may also use a cloth tape binding as an artificial selvage to reduce the likelihood of tension rips.

Problem 7: *The ink spills over the back side of the frame when the screen is raised.*

Possible Cause A—The screen is raised at too steep an angle.

Suggested Remedy—Either don't raise the screen quite so high, or else prop up the back end of the printing bed.

Possible Cause B—The frame isn't deep enough for the amount of ink carried in the screen.

Suggested Remedy—Build up the backside of the frame with a cardboard strip that turns partly into the sides, creating a high trough. Better still, limit the amount of ink carried in the screen.

Problem 8: *Every precaution has been taken to control the register—hinges tightened, guides checked, cleats nailed to the printing bed to prevent shifting of screen frame—yet there's a consistent movement of the printed image, alternating between right and left.*

Possible Cause A—The normal pressure of the squeegee as it's pushed from one side of the screen to the other may produce an imperceptible shift of the screen fabric. This occurs when the fabric isn't as tautly stretched as it should be.

Suggested Remedy—Keep right and left impressions in separate stacks throughout the run on all colors, or squeegee the entire edition in one direction only. (In the future, do a better job of stretching the screen fabric.)

Possible Cause B—Weather has a hydrostatic effect on the screen fabric, especially when the stencil is made with glue or another water-soluble emulsion. Excessive humidity relaxes the tension of the fabric, resulting in a movement of the printed image as the squeegee is passed back and forth.

Suggested Remedy—Place the screen in front of an electric heater to remove accumulated moisture. Within minutes, the fabric will become taut again.

Problem 9: *The printing bed has developed a slight warp, creating an uneven printing surface, even though it's constructed of seasoned lumber and well protected with a coat of lacquer.*

Possible Cause—The bed may have been stored in a leaning position for an extended period of time.

Suggested Remedy—The warp may be partially or completely corrected by fastening two wood or metal crossbars (one at each end) to the underside of the bed.

Stencil Preparation

Problem 10: *In the process of cutting a paper stencil, the island parts curl and tend to shift out of position.*

Possible Cause—Most likely the paper used for the stencil was taken from a tightly wound roll.

Suggested Remedy—In cutting the stencil, leave tiny uncut nicks strategically positioned to keep the island parts down and in place. The nicks will easily give way when the stencil is stripped, after it's adhered to the screen. You can avoid this problem by using paper in sheet rather than in roll form.

Problem 11: *When adhering handcut film stencils to the screen, some of the film edges break down and dissolve.*

Possible Cause A—There's poor contact between screen fabric and film. This allows the fabric to move up and down as the film is wetted and dried, thereby producing an abrasive action which dissolves or "burns" the film edges.

Suggested Remedy—To assure better contact, bear down on the screen frame as you adhere the stencil, or else, place several layers of cardboard underneath the film to serve as a pack-up.

Possible Cause B—You're using a faulty adhering technique. Rubbing too hard, using an excessive amount of thinner, or not following quickly enough with a dry cloth rub will ruin the film edges.

Suggested Remedy—Just a slight moistening with the adhering fluid and a gentle wiping motion with a dry cloth is the prescribed technique for successful adhering. The faster the fluid is removed after it's applied to the screen, the sharper the film edges will be.

Possible Cause C—You're pressing down too hard with the stencil knife. This produces deep grooves in the backing sheet in which the adhering fluid is trapped. This will dissolve the edges of the film. Also if the stencil knife is held at a bevel, the blade will lift the film edges, thus destroying the perfect contact that good adhering requires.

Suggested Remedy—The blade of the stencil knife should be razor sharp, making it unnecessary to apply pressure when cutting. To avoid cutting at a bevel, the stencil knife should be held almost upright, with the tip of the blade at a right angle to the surface of the film.

Possible Cause D—The film surface is dusty, greasy, or kinked, especially in the vicinity of the design image.

Suggested Remedy—To reduce the incidence of burned edges, it's of utmost importance to protect the film against grease, smudges, and other damage before and after it's cut.

Problem 12: *In making a stencil with the photographic method, and quite often with the handcut method too, as the backing sheet is removed, some of the detail of the stencil image comes off with it.*

Possible Cause A—There's poor contact between film and screen fabric during adhering.

Suggested Remedy—If the backing sheet shows the slightest resistance when it's pulled away from the film tissue, stop. Re-adhere it using a pack-up of sufficient thickness to improve the contact.

Possible Cause B—The backing sheet is removed too soon, before the film has had a chance to dry.

Suggested Remedy—Allow ample time for the film tissue to dry thoroughly. A fan will hasten the process. When dry, the backing sheet of a well adhered stencil will come off without resistance, and without disturbing the finest detail of the stencil image. There's no harm at all in letting the film dry "too long."

Problem 13: *The photostencil develops numerous pinholes within a short time, although the manufacturer's data sheet states that the stencil will hold up well for long runs.*

Possible Cause—Exposure time is too short. One of the symptoms of underexposure is a thin, weak stencil tissue that breaks down easily.

Suggested Remedy—Normally a more substantial stencil tissue requires proportionately longer exposure.

Remember that exposure schedules indicated in manufacturers' data sheets are intended to be flexible, since many variables must be considered—nature and intensity of the light source and its distance from the sensitized surface, the character of the positive, etc. Because of these variables it is good practice to make exposure tests.

Problem 14: *In the preparation of a photostencil, after the design image is washed out, some of the* fine lines don't open at all; others have narrowed down considerably.

Possible Cause A—The film is overexposed.

Suggested Remedy—At this stage, this condition may only be partially corrected by an additional wash with a more forceful spray of water. Next time, run an exposure test before proceeding.

Possible Cause B—Imperfect contact between sensitized surface and positive during exposure allows the light to undercut the opaque areas of the design image.

Suggested Remedy—An extra washing will be of some help. In the future, see to it that the positive and sensitized surface are in the closest contact possible.

Problem 15: *In masking out the open screen area with fill-in compound, some of it seeps through the screen, forming globules.*

Possible Cause A—This is more likely to happen when a brush is used. In applying the compound to the surface of the screen, the bristles of the brush tend to push it through the mesh in spots.

Suggested Remedy—You get much better results (and it's faster too) by applying fill-in compound with a sharp-edged piece of stiff cardboard, celluloid triangle, or a commercial scraper, used in the manner of a squeegee. For a second coat, if that is desired, a brush may be used safely.

Possible Cause B—The fill-in compound has been thinned too much.

Suggested Remedy—Add heavier fill-in compound and mix thoroughly.

Problem 16: *In washing out the design image of a tusche-glue stencil, some of the fine lines and subtle texture areas don't open completely.*

Possible Cause A—The tusche isn't applied heavily enough to fill the mesh. A mere surface impression lacks sufficient body to act as an effective resist for the glue.

Suggested Remedy—Soaking the underside of the screen with kerosene or other tusche solvent for an extended period of time will help. In addition, it may also be necessary to use a small bristle brush to dislodge stubborn areas which haven't completely dissolved.

Possible Cause B—The glue coating is thicker than it should be, thus forming a crust-like film over the tusche, which is hard to break down.

Suggested Remedy—Same as for *Possible Cause A*.

Possible Cause C—The screen wasn't kept level when the glue coating was applied. This caused the glue to drift partially into the tusched area on the underside of the screen, thus trapping the tusche between two layers of glue.

Suggested Remedy—Once this occurs, it'll take lots of soaking with solvent and a vigorous brushing to open the affected areas of the design image.

Problem 17: *When handcut film is positioned over the art, some of the colors of the art aren't distinguishable with sufficient clarity for accurate color separation during the cutting of the stencil.*

Possible Cause—The stencil film acts as a color filter, thus weakening or canceling out its corresponding color on the art.

Suggested Remedy—Since stencil film comes in a number of different colors, select a color which will least conflict with those on the art. Another suggestion is to outline the boundaries of the colors on the art, using a soft, drawing pencil. When the film is placed over the art, the color boundaries will easily be distinguishable by the reflection of the pencil outlines as they're seen through the film.

Register

Problem 18: *When printing on freshly purchased cardboard and paper stock, register varies considerably from one day to the next.*

Possible Cause—The stock hasn't had a chance to rid itself of moisture acquired in the process of manufacture.

Suggested Remedy—Where close register is important, it's good practice to "season" fresh stock prior to printing, by exposing the stock to the air. Place the individual sheets on open racks or tables for several hours, overnight, or longer.

Problem 19: *An irregularity in register unnoticed in the printing of the first color is discovered when the second color is printed, making it difficult to get the colors to align.*

Possible Cause—Irregularity in register may be attributed to any of a number of factors: carelessness in feeding, faulty guides, side-to-side movement of the screen frame, loose hinges, dimensional instability of the stock or the stencil, etc.

Suggested Remedy—Under the circumstances, color registration can still be controlled by resorting to a flap guide device instead of the standard fixed guide system. A sheet of transparent acetate on which a master impression of the second color is printed is fastened to the bed in such a manner that it can be folded back and forth like a page in a book. Register is established by visually positioning the stock under the acetate so that the design image on the stock and the acetate align. The acetate is then folded back and the print made. Once the setup is established, register can be controlled for the duration of the edition.

Inks

Note: Although the various problems on inks referred to here allude specifically to oil based paints, they apply in equal measure to other ink formulations as well.

Problem 20: *During the course of printing, the paint heavies up in the screen, making it difficult to push it through the mesh.*

Possible Cause—Too much paint is carried at one time. With the constant movement of the squeegee, the unused paint in the screen tends to thicken as the volatile solvents evaporate.

Suggested Remedy—Limit the quantity of paint carried in the screen so that you have enough for twenty to fifty impressions, depending upon the surface area being printed.

Problem 21: *The paint dries into the screen, clogging the mesh.*

Possible Cause A—Assuming that the right type of paint is used for the job on hand, the clogging may be due to the indiscriminate use of naphtha, turpentine, benzine, or a similar highly volatile solvent as a thinning agent.

Suggested Remedy—Remove the paint and wash the screen. Add a slow drying varnish to the paint mixture to counteract the presence of the volatile solvents, and resume printing.

Possible Cause B—A current of air blowing in the direction of the screen tends to make the paint dry into the mesh.

Suggested Remedy—Avoid working near an open window or a fan.

Problem 22: *Although the printed sheets feel dry to the touch before they are collected, they offset or stick together when stacked in a pile.*

Possible Cause—The layer of paint (apparently dry on the surface) may still have trapped solvents underneath which cannot escape when the sheets are stacked on top of each other prematurely. As a consequence, the paint is rewetted, causing it to stick or offset.

Suggested Remedy—Check the degree of drying by digging a fingernail into the surface of the print. If the paint feels soft underneath, allow more time for drying. As a safeguard against the possibility of offsetting or sticking, keep the stacks low, especially if the prints are to be stored for extended periods.

(Right) Communication Series #5. No Sooner is the Word Spoken by J. I. Biegeleisen, edition 45. The sequence of color printings here was: light gray, dark gray, red, and black. Of these the first three colors were printed with handcut paper stencils; black, the final color in the sequence, was printed with a handcut film stencil.

Ceramic Mug. *The colorful design decorating this mug was screened with special ceramic inks which upon firing fuse with the surface.*

Dish Towel. *Decorative towels such as the ones shown can be screen printed with simple equipment at home or in the workshop.*

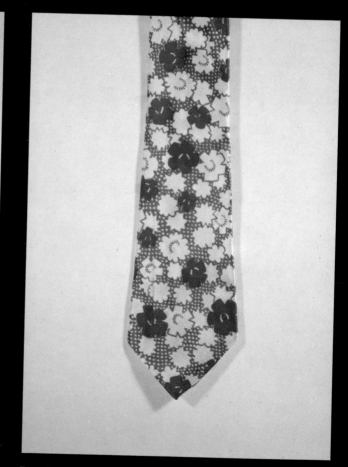

Greeting Card. *The choice of stock for printing greeting cards by the screen process includes a great variety of papers, bristol boards, and metallic foils.*

Tie. *Designs on ties and scarves (printed in single or multiple units) may be applied with the same basic equipment used in dress goods and other softwear.*

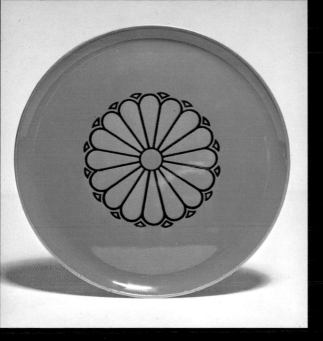

Tray. *Many of the colorful trays so popular today are printed by the screen process.*

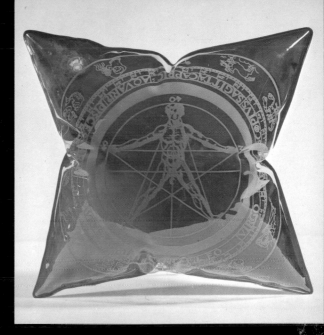

Inflatable Pillow. *The growing popularity of inflatable products such as this pillow provides new business opportunities for the screen printer.*

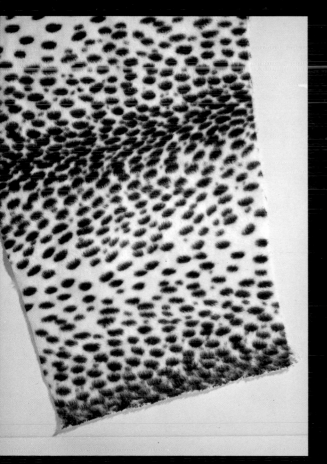

Simulated Fur. *Exotic furs are remarkably well simulated by screen printing spots, stripes, etc. on inexpensive domestic animal skins and acrylic cloth.*

Tote Bag. *The vinyl tote bag shown was screen printed with synthetic inks formulated for maximum adhesion and flexibility.*

Printing

Problem 23: *The squeegee jumps and is deflected as it hits the edge of the stock being printed, often causing trouble in printing and damage to the screen fabric.*

Possible Cause—This sometimes occurs when the stock is heavy, especially if it's a hard surface material such as glass or metal.

Suggested Remedy—Build up the surface of the bed surrounding the stock with layers of cardboard to the level of the stock being printed. The squeegee will then have a smooth surface to ride on.

Problem 24: *When printing on thin paper stock, it clings to the underside of the screen after each impression, blurring as it's pulled away.*

Possible Cause A—The paint is too thick.

Suggested Remedy—Dilute the paint to a more fluid consistency.

Possible Cause B—The paper is attracted to the screen by static electricity produced by the action of the squeegee as it crosses the screen.

Suggested Remedy—There are a number of suggestions.

(1) Place several pieces of doubleface tape on the bed within the margin area of the printing image. The doubleface tape will hold the paper to the bed when the screen is lifted.
(2) Place a thin strip of wood or cardboard under the front end of the screen frame. In this way, just as soon as the squeegee passes over the printing surface, the screen fabric will pull away, leaving the paper on the bed.
(3) Use a number of small ⅛" self-adhesive rubber disks (such as Dr. Scholl's corn pads), strategically positioning them on the underside of the screen away from the design image. The screen fabric will automatically lift off the printing surface, in the same manner as above.

Problem 25: *In the course of printing, leaks develop along the inside edges of the screen where fabric and frame meet.*

Possible Cause—The gum paper binding hasn't been applied properly. As a result, the paint trapped in pockets ultimately oozes out during printing.

Suggested Remedy—Remove the paint; wash the screen, and dry it thoroughly. Rebind the edges, making doubly sure that the gum paper strips stick firmly and evenly.

(Left) This section of decoratively patterned wallpaper was screened on washable paper with special fadeproof lacquer inks. The design was printed with six handcut lacquerproof film stencils. Courtesy Paint Print Process Co., New York.

Problem 26: *The paint dries unevenly, with some areas on the print taking longer to dry than others.*

Possible Cause A—There are depressions on the surface of the printing bed.

Suggested Remedy—If the depressions aren't too pronounced, they can be leveled off by filling the affected areas with plastic wood. In other cases, it would be better to cover the bed with a sheet of heavy, smooth cardboard.

Possible Cause B—There's a low spot in the squeegee blade.

Suggested Remedy—Sand down the squeegee blade and check it against a plate glass or other surface known to be absolutely level.

Possible Cause C—There are variations in squeegee pressure, resulting in uneven paint distribution.

Suggested Remedy—Make an effort to apply even pressure on the squeegee throughout the edition.

Possible Cause D—The paint isn't completely mixed; some parts are more viscous than others.

Suggested Remedy—Remove the paint and mix it thoroughly to be sure that solvents and other ingredients are uniformly interspersed.

Problem 27: *In bearing down on the squeegee, the rubber blade bends noticeably, and fails to push the ink through properly.*

Possible Cause A—Too much pressure is applied to the squeegee.

Suggested Remedy—Lighten the pressure but distribute the force evenly. In most instances, the weight of the squeegee and the hand holding it will exert sufficient pressure to push the paint through the openings of the stencil.

Possible Cause B—The rubber blade is either too soft or lacks the required thickness.

Suggested Remedy—Use a good grade of natural or synthetic rubber, not departing too much from the ⅜" thickness generally recommended for commercial work.

Possible Cause C—The paint mixture is too thick.

Suggested Remedy—Thin the consistency of the paint with a compatible reducing agent.

Problem 28: *A streak on the print shows up with each scrape of the squeegee.*

Possible Cause A—If the streak appears consistently in the same place, it may be due to a nick in the squeegee rubber or a configuration on the surface of the bed.

Suggested Remedy—Correct the condition, whichever it may be.

Possible Cause B—If the position of the streak varies from print to print, it may be due to flecks of un-diluted components in the paint which have not been completely dispersed.

Suggested Remedy—Remove the paint, stir it thoroughly and as an added precaution, strain it through a fine metal sieve or a double layer of cheesecloth.

Problem 29: *Paper and other thin stock catch on the bed when fed into the guides.*

Possible Cause—The printing bed is either sticky or abrasive.

Suggested Remedy—With a soft rag or powder puff, rub a little talcum on the bed, or else cover the surface with a sheet of acetate or smooth cardboard.

Problem 30: *When printing a solid coating of color, the paint runs off the edges of the stock, smudging the printing bed.*

Possible Cause—No allowance was made for the slight spread of color or for possible variations in the size of the stock.

Suggested Remedy—Cut the stock larger to begin with, and then trim it to size after printing. This will not only prevent smudging the printing bed, but will provide an adequate margin for handling the stock in feeding and take-off.

Problem 31: *When printing metallic colors such as gold and silver, difficulty is encountered in pushing the paint through the mesh.*

Possible Cause—The bronzing powders used in metallic paints are generally not as finely ground as the pigment particles in standard inks and as such don't penetrate the mesh as easily.

Suggested Remedy—To get a good penetration of metallic paints, avoid using a mesh finer than #12. A #10XX silk or equivalent fabric is recommended.

CHAPTER FIFTEEN

Diversified opportunities in screen printing, as a craft and business

You see evidence of screen printing all about you: at home, on the flocked wallpaper that adds a note of Old World elegance to the living room décor, the vinyl shower curtains, guest towels, tablecloths, drapes, glassware, and tea trays. At school you see it in the distinctive typographic designs on textbook covers, instruction charts, and other graphic visual aids. Most likely the flag in the classroom, pennants and insignias on T-shirts and jackets are also screen printed. At the office, the dial on the large office clock, the trademark on the Coke machine, the shade on the table lamp in the reception room, the corporate seal on the rug—all are (or could be) produced by this most versatile of all printing processes.

The commercial applications of the process are so diverse that no one single screen printing establishment (no matter how well equipped it may be) could possibly handle the full range of products and materials to which the process can be applied. It's customary, therefore, for many firms to specialize in one or a limited number of select areas.

The following is an overview of some of the major areas of specialization.

Signs and Posters

The production of commercial signs and posters constitutes the backbone of the screen printing industry in terms of total number of people employed, output measured by annual dollar volume of business, and number of individual entrepreneurs who operate their own businesses. The size of screen printing businesses ranges from the one-man vest-pocket shops to fully staffed firms of fifty or more employees which include a retinue of designers, letterers, stencilmakers, printers, and sales representatives.

Within the large field of sign and poster printing, there are ever so many subspecialties. There are shops that specialize in printing paper signs and display cards for the chainstore, supermarket, and department store trade; others go in for the design and production of bus cards, window displays, or advertising banners. Some of the larger shops are set up specifically for twenty-four sheet billboard posters. These are usually printed in sections which when mounted in proper sequence appear as giant display bulletins on highways and city streets. There are firms whose main business is the production of signs on glass, metal, or plastics. A growing number of firms working in close cooperation with prominent artists and designers have developed a profitable specialty in the production of decorative posters (such as those by Peter Max) for home and office interiors.

Greeting Cards

Screen printing of greeting cards can be big business or can be purposely limited to a restricted output. There are a number of large firms which specialize in screened greeting cards, with facilities for national distribution; others confine both their creative and production efforts to custom-made designs. On a limited scale, the screening of greeting cards can be carried on with the simplest type of hand-operated equipment and with comparatively little work space. On a mass production basis, screening is usually done with high-speed automatic presses capable of several thousand impressions per hour. During the peak of the season these presses are kept in high gear for weeks on end.

Among the successful entrepreneurs of screen printed greeting cards are those who first turned to the process as a means of "doing their own Christmas cards"; they soon found a ready market for their creative efforts, which they hadn't anticipated at the outset. Their expanded line of greeting cards, now widely distributed, includes hundreds of designs appropriate for every festivity and occasion.

Decorative Gift Wrap Papers

It is customary for greeting card manufacturers to put out a coordinated line of gift wraps appropriate for seasonal greetings and special occasions— Christmas, Easter, Valentine's Day, anniversaries, birthdays, weddings, engagements, etc. Often, the better type of gift wraps calling for limited editions of exclusive designs are reserved for the screen process. It's the most expedient way of applying

Designed as a point-of-purchase attraction for gas stations, this die-cut outdoor "pole" display was screened on waterproof board with inks that successfully withstand all weather conditions. Courtesy Process Displays, Inc., New Berlin, Wisconsin.

Here's that Tiger!

pure opaque colors in full brilliance to any stock. Many of the designs are screened with light colored inks on shiny black flint and other stock, as well as on gold and silver foils, and other exotic papers.

In addition to printing exclusive designs for gift wraps, there's a market for screened and flocked papers as decorative coverings and "liners" for boxes and containers used in the cosmetic packaging field.

Book Covers

Screening on book covers has become a specialty for a number of firms who have established a good working relationship with publishers and bookbinders. The versatile nature of the process which makes it possible to print on almost any kind of stock —pyroxylin-coated cloth, vinyl, and buckram—has created a field for screen printing not in direct competition with other processes. This is most often the case where short run editions and special bindings are needed.

Cover designs on rebound books intended for library and school use are frequently printed by the screen process in bright, gay colors which appeal to young readers.

Screen printing is also done on covers and special inserts for souvenir journals, school yearbooks, annual reports, and in some instances, on covers for advertising brochures and decorative menus.

Art Prints

Every artist printmaker hopes to have his work eagerly sought out and distributed by important art dealers and galleries. A select few have achieved that distinction, and nearly all their creations, which bear their signature, are sold at fabulous prices. By and large, however, the average artist-printmaker who intends to make multiple reproductions of his work his sole or even supplementary source of income must look towards a less lofty but wider market for his creative output. One such market, which has been on the ascendancy in recent years, is supplying the hotel and motel franchise organizations with framable screen prints. This market provides the artist-printmaker with an opportunity for greater exposure of his talents, while at the same time engaging in a profitable enterprise.

A number of large firms specializing in this area of screen printing had their beginnings as one-man studio workshops. Now they combine screening and framemaking, working closely with national distributors of pictures for the hotel, motel, and home decoration trade.

Lampshades

Screening on lampshades calls for no special equipment other than that needed for general poster printing. Usually lampshades are printed on flat

Many three dimensional displays that you see in windows and interiors of stores are produced by the screen printing process. Courtesy Hutcheson Process Displays, Omaha, Nebraska.

The screen process lends itself admirably to the application of lettering and design on a variety of cover stock used in book production. Courtesy Process Displays, Inc., New Berlin, Wisconsin.

sheets, after which they're die-cut to shape and assembled. In most instances, smaller-size shades are "ganged up," two or more on a sheet, to effect economy in the printing and finishing operations.

The screen process is inherently suited for printing on lampshade material since it can be used with equal ease on parchment, silk, vinyl, or whatever else the specifications call for. The ink can be formulated to be compatible with any choice of stock and to resist heat and fading. Though most lampshades are printed with transparent or translucent colors, it's feasible to use inks which are totally lightproof. In this latter respect, the screen printing process is unique among all other printing methods, because complete opacity can be achieved with just one impression.

Screen printing firms, who service the lampshade manufacturing industry, find there's a sufficient demand for their specialty to employ a full complement of designers, stencilmakers, and printers the year round.

Charts and Presentation Books

Since the screen process is one of the most economical methods for color printing of limited editions, the process has become the major method for the reproduction of sales charts, presentation books, multicolor graphs, and related visual aid material. These are produced on paper or thin board, on flexible vinyl or transparent acetate, on cloth, or any other material suited for the purpose, and in sizes as small as the pages of this book or as large as a wall.

There are a number of firms (identifed in the trade as chartmakers or presentation houses) in every large city who have gained pre-eminence as specialists in the production of visual aid material of this kind.

Rugs and Carpeting

The printing of colorful designs on rugs and carpeting by means of the screen process—an innovative approach to decorative floor covering—is a relatively new trade specialty. The process makes it practical to produce custom-made patterns in units or in continuous yardage at a price considerably lower than other conventional methods, and with color effects uniquely its own.

The size of the printing area can vary from a small welcome mat to 12'-wide broadloom carpeting. Screen units are built to accommodate whatever size is required. Colors are matched to the customer's exact specifications.

Measured by the success of the increasing number of firms (large and small) which have embarked in this specialty, it's evident that there's an existing and growing demand for custom-made, screen printed floor coverings to reflect shifting trends in interior decoration.

Bottles and other Containers

Product identifications screen printed directly on bottles, jars, and other containers are rapidly replacing conventional labels. This is especially true of beverages, cosmetics, and household products packaged in glass or polyethylene containers.

Screening on containerware has evolved into a distinct field of operation quite separate and apart from routine screen printing. Bottle plants operate their own screen printing departments at the point of manufacture, to avoid the expense and potential damage entailed in packing and shipping.

Container marking and decoration are done on a mass production basis with automatic screen printing presses, and related drying equipment engineered specifically for the product printed. Geared to high-speed production, these presses are capable of handling more than 5,000 units per hour on a continuing basis. In most cases, special enamel inks are employed, which upon baking fuse with the surface on which the design is applied.

Tumblers and other Kitchen Glassware

The chances are that the decorative motifs on those bright-colored drinking glasses that grace your breakfast table have been printed by the screen process. Indeed, there's no more economical and effective way to print colors on glass.

Like bottle and container printing, commercial screening on tumblers, jars, cups, and similar glassware has become a big production business, calling for high-speed presses to make it a profitable venture. The inks used are, for the most part, of the ceramic type, which require firing to assure maximum adhesion and enduring color fastness.

For limited editions, such glassware may be screen printed with simple jigs alluded to in Chapter 12. These can be purchased at major screen supply dealers.

Trays and Placemats

The printing of trays and placemats, which constitutes a secondary specialty for a number of commercial screen shops, has particular appeal to the small group of designers and printmakers who cater to a limited but exclusive clientele. They command good prices for their creative efforts.

Trays are usually printed with high gloss lacquers or enamels. The colors are bright, permanent, and have excellent resistance to detergents and alcohols. When preshaped with a lip or upturn at the sides, trays are printed with screens either shaped to fit the contour, or small enough to fit the shallow, flat area. Sometimes decals are used which are transferred into position and covered with a heavy coating of transparent varnish, lacquer, or enamel. In large-scale commercial printing, trays are often handled as flat sheets ganged up in multiples. Later they're cut, molded, or otherwise shaped by die-cutting and stamping.

The printing of placemats involves no unusual screen equipment. There's a wide choice of surfaces to select from—wood, cork, plastic, rubber composition, pyroxylin-coated paper and cloth, straw sheets, and many others. Each of these calls for a carefully selected, compatible ink formulation.

Flocked Products

While many screen shops will, on occasion, do flocking in conjunction with their regular work, flocking on a full-time production basis has become a major field of specialization in screen printing.

No doubt you've seen flock used on many surfaces—wallpaper, T-shirts, game cloths, banners, dress material, greeting cards, window displays, and toys. However, you may not have associated any of these with screen printing. There are, of course, other methods employed in flocking, but by and large, the screen process has proven itself to be superior to any other. One of the determining factors in successful flocking is the adhesive; the heavier it is, the better it will hold the flock. The nature of the screen process is such that the amount of adhesive passing through the screen can be regulated by the size of the mesh and the selection of the squeegee. To get a heavier and more viscous deposit a coarser mesh (#8 or #10) and/or a softer squeegee can be used.

Essentially, flock consists of finely cut strands of cotton, rayon, silk, or other fibers. When these are sprinkled by sieve, shot through a spray nozzle, or otherwise applied to a tacky surface, they adhere to it. Then they impart to the surface a fuzzy-textured appearance, like suede, plush, or velvet. The final result depends upon the size and the kind of flock used. Flock comes in many different colors including brilliant fluorescents, and in lengths ranging from less than 1/50" to 1/4"; the most popular lengths are 1/16" and 1/32".

Flock can be applied as an all-over covering, or in controlled areas as needed. Regular-type stencils are used. The adhesive is squeegeed onto the surface of the stock in the same manner as standard ink. While the adhesive is still wet, the flock is applied, then shaken off to remove the excess. In small quantity production, the flocking can be done by hand, but it's more expedient to use one of the commercial flocking machines when a level of full-scale production is reached. Among the later developments in technical equipment for flocking is a self-contained unit which operates on the electrostatic principle. This puts on the flock and removes the excess electrostatically, all in an enclosed chamber, and at production speeds far beyond the capability of hand-operated methods.

In a like manner, the screen process is used for applying adhesives for tinsel, sparkle dust, and other reflective appliqué effects.

Simulated Furs

Another novel application of the screen process is the printing of simulated furs. The "fur" look is achieved by stenciling spots, stripes, and other characteristic animal markings on the comparatively inexpensive skins of sheep, rabbits, and goats. That smart leopard fur that milady's coat is made of may not have come from a ferocious leopard at all, but from the tender hide of a nannygoat. In some instances, the "fur" may consist of flock-treated acrylic cloth, screen printed with deep penetrating dye compounds to take on the texture and coloration of whatever fur style reflects the vogue of the season.

Screen printed simulated furs of one kind or another are also used for hats, muffs, handbags, and other accessories, as well as for throw rugs, and decorative seatcover material. Next time you visit a posh nightclub and find yourself seated on a luxurious zebra patterned lounge, you may suspect (not without some justification) that those zebra stripes were put there by screen and squeegee.

Wallpaper

No one who visits a large showroom of a major wallpaper house can help being impressed by the spectacular array of colorful patterns—stripes, florals, period styles, abstracts, and scenics. Likely as not, a good portion of the collection, particularly those on vinyl and metallic foils, were printed by the screen process. Assuredly, that's the case with nearly all flocked patterns.

The screen printing process, with particular reference to wallpaper, has a number of outstanding advantages in its favor. It's possible to print a light color over a dark ground when the design calls for it. In most instances, it's less expensive especially for short run editions. Stencils cost far less to prepare than the printing plates used in gravure and other conventional methods. Then too, colors can be as bright as the designer wishes them to be, with total effects that come closer to hand painting than is possible with any other commercial printing process.

In some ways, screening on wallpaper is similar to screening on textiles. Indeed, some wallpapers are of fabric composition. The printing can be done with hinged screens or on long, open tables, the same as those used for textiles. The production setup can be inexpensive, and portable. It can be confined to the improvised facilities of a home studio or small workshop, or expanded to a large-scale enterprise requiring elaborate facilities and prodigious floor space.

Printers of wallpaper don't, as a rule, have to contend with curing and other complex postprinting treatments associated with textile printing. But wallpaper printers (whether using screen or any other method) have to contend with unique problems indigenous to their own craft. These include retention of absolute color uniformity throughout the edition, and precision register control to assure faultless pattern matching. There are other technical disciplines. Inks must be made to dry with sufficient flexibility to permit tight rolling; they mustn't bleed through to the underside. This would cause an oily surface which would interfere with water pastes. Of course, these inks must be fadeproof.

Wallpapers are printed in cut sections (like piece goods) or in continuous rolls. Standard roll widths are 18", 22", 24", and 30"; the latter is the most prevalent. Sections in large widths are printed (usually in limited editions) as "scenics." When placed on the wall in proper sequence, they appear as continuous pictorial murals.

Within the wallpaper printing industry, there are firms that specialize in custom-made prints on a restricted edition basis only, catering to a select clientele. Others are set up for large-scale production and mass distribution, with outlets which include department stores, household furnishing shops, and painters' and decorators' supply stores. Confined to limited quantities, custom-made wallpapers can be screened with a minimal investment in equipment. They offer the enterprising designer-printer excellent prospects for a creative and profitable business venture; exclusive designs bring high prices.

Textiles

Screen printing on textiles, if operated on an extensive scale, can take on the dimensions of a million-dollar business. The setup for quantity production costs many thousands of dollars for equipment and an enormous amount of work space. Open printing tables alone can cost anywhere from $3,000 to $10,000 each, depending upon length and type of construction. Large establishments have a battery of them with equally extensive (and expensive) facilities for drying and curing treatments. But with textile screen printing as with other specialties of the process, it's possible to gear the scope and production technique to suit your personal preference and objectives.

It would be difficult to categorize the great diversity of fabrics and end products in the broad area of the textile decorating field that lend themselves to screen printing. Dress goods, toweling, drapery and upholstery material, tablecloths and napkins, cloths used for shirtings, lounge and sleepwear—these represent only a partial listing suggestive of the material and products that can be printed by the process.

Until recently, one of the technical drawbacks to the screen printing of textiles, as a home or studio craft, was the comparative lack of commercially available textile inks. Established textile screen printers had for years formulated their own at considerable cost to themselves, and were naturally reluctant to share their knowledge with competitors in the field, large or small. Today, with the easy availability of commercial emulsions and other ink formulations, screening on textiles has opened new possibilities for home craftsmen, designers, and others who wish to enter the field, either on a limited or full-scale production basis.

Decals

Nearly everybody, since early childhood, is familiar with decals. Short for decalcomanias, a decal is a printed image which is slid off, or otherwise transferred, from a backing sheet to another surface. The decal print takes the contour of the surface to which it's applied and, for all practical purposes, becomes a part of that surface. Commercially, decals are used as a transfer medium for applying lettering or design on store windows, truck bodies, vending machines, walls, and on any flat or curved surfaces which cannot conveniently be printed or painted on directly.

The screen process is by no means the only method by which decals are produced. Decals were in use long before the screen process was perfected. The art of making decals was first developed in Europe in the latter part of the 19th century. Women would gather in sewing-circle-type meetings and spread glue coatings over thin paper sheets. On top of the coatings they would apply a clear varnish to form a transparent film. They would then paint their designs on the film surface. After immersing these sheets in water to dissolve the glue, they were able to transfer the designs to pottery, glasses, dishes, and other kitchenware. These early progenitors of decal art worked with such enthusiasm that they were collectively (and good humoredly) referred to in the community as "decalcomaniacs"—the last three syllables meaning the enthusiastic ones or "the mad ones." Later decal making was put on a more commercial basis and printed by lithography, a process which still is one of the principle methods used in the production of decals. During the course of time, however, the screen printing process has proven itself strongly competitive, and in many ways superior to lithography. Technically speaking, it's by far the most practical way to apply a heavy deposit of varnish or lacquer—one with sufficient body and flexibility to produce a film easily transferable from a backing sheet to a receiving surface.

There are four main types of decals: the Simplex, the Duplex, Pressure-Sensitive Slide-off, and the Dry type. With the Simplex, also called the Slide-off type, the design image is slid off the backing sheet face down or face up; in the Duplex, the design is applied face down only. The Pressure-Sensitive Slide-off type, is one where the design is applied face down or face up; the Dry type likewise is applied face down or face up. Special paper is used for each type of decal. Data sheets describing the various printing and transfer procedures are available from the manufacturer.

The printing of decals has grown into a distinct and important segment of the screen printing industry with special facilities and high-speed automatic equipment needed for large-scale production.

Printed Circuits

Screen printed circuits were first used during World War II by the U.S. Army in the production of miniaturized circuitry for the "proximity fuse" which proved so effective in aerial warfare. The commercial possibilities for printed circuitry were soon recognized by a number of radio and T.V. manufacturers. In 1948 they jointly decided to develop this method, hopefully planning to replace, or at least to reduce, costly and time-consuming operations involved in hand wiring. Their most sanguine anticipations were realized. They found the screen process to be the most adaptable of methods whereby circuits could be manufactured on a mass production basis. It became apparent that the screen process offered the best means of applying heavy deposits of conductive inks and resist compounds necessary for the production of printed circuits.

The impact that screen printed circuits had on the electronic industry was immediate, and a new specialty was born for screen printers—one which has grown enormously through the years.

Screen printed circuitry is now universally used not only in radio and television sets, but in aerospace components, computers, business machines, clocks, kitchen appliances, recorders, hearing aids, and has all but replaced conventional hand wiring. Printed circuits have more than mere economy to recommend them. They make it possible to achieve uniformity in mass produced electronic components and instrumentation, and permit infinitely greater range in miniaturization. The screening of printed circuits, by any of the means described below, constitutes a full-time venture for a growing number of shops throughout the United States and abroad.

There are three basic methods of producing printed circuits by the screen process: (1) the *conductive ink* method, (2) the *etching* method, and (3) the *plating* method.

The conductive ink method: This is the simplest of the three. Here a stencil is made (either handcut, or photographic) representing the schematic pattern of the circuit. The inks used are specially formulated lacquers or oil based paints. These are composed of a conductive metallic compound suspended in a compatible liquid to form a printable paste. Since silver and copper are excellent conductors of electricity, either of these metals, used alone or in compounds as oxides or nitrates, are most commonly employed. The printing procedure is the same as for routine poster printing, except that the printing stock isn't the usual cardboard or paper, but mica, Pyrex, porcelain, or other refractory nonconductors. Where a specially heavy deposit of conductive ink is called for (as is often the case), a comparatively coarse screen mesh is used. For the very fine lines and extremely close tolerance required for miniaturized circuitry, a relatively fine mesh is necessary. Postprint treatment usually includes baking to assure maximum adhesion and durability.

The printing of electronic circuits by the screen process has now reached the proportion of a major field of specialization.

The etching method: Here the printing medium is an acid etch resist compound prepared in paste form. This resist compound is printed in the form of the schematic pattern of the circuit, on a metal-clad laminate. This is a sheet of copper, aluminum, or other good conductive metal laminated to a panel board made of a nonconductive material such as phenolic plastic. The metal-clad laminate is then immersed in a solution of ferric chloride or similar etching compound. The parts protected by the resist compound (the lines comprising the printed circuit) as well as the phenolic plastic panel board are immune to the compound. Only the exposed metal surface is affected. This etches away. The resist coating is then removed—a procedure easily accomplished with a degreaser or solvent. When that's done, the metal lines of the circuit appear in relief on the plastic panel board which acts as a base.

The plating method: Here the entire area of a nonconductive surface is screened with a resist *except* for the lines representing the schematic circuit. The surface is then subjected to a plating process which deposits a layer of copper, silver, tin, lead, or other highly conductive metal on the exposed lines. When the resist is subsequently removed, the schematic pattern of the circuit in plated metal appears in bold relief on the nonconductive support.

In the final fabrication, regardless of the method used, the required electric components are attached to the board—a phase of production which doesn't fall within the province of the screen printer.

Conclusion

This overview of the diverse fields of specialization encompasses at best only a partial listing of the many practical applications of screen printing. The screen process is so flexible that new uses are found for it every day—some most unique. A case in point is the large baking company—a leader in its field—which has recently adapted the process for "printing" floral decorations and other design configurations for its "special occasion" party cakes. This is accomplished by screening a heavy deposit of an edible vegetable dye emulsion (in color) on a thin sugar-based disk which is subsequently transferred to the cake. In the process of baking, the emulsion swells forming a sculptural configuration; the disk having fulfilled its function as a carrier, melts inconspicuously into the body of the cake.

Experimentation is currently going on in developing aromatic ink compounds, which when printed onto a surface would impart to it a lasting fragrance. The merchandising psychology "if you can smell it—you can sell it" has been tested in the field. There it was found to have an impelling sales appeal in advertising products such as coffee, citrus fruits, perfumes, and flowers. With the screen process, more than any other form of printing, it's possible to get a high ink build up, which has a direct relation to the lasting qualities of the fragrance. It may very well be that yet another area of specialization is soon to be added to this, the most adaptable of all printing processes in existence.

Screen printing can be "big business" as indicated by this view of a section of the production department of a large commercial shop. Courtesy Process Displays, Inc., New Berlin, Wisconsin.

Glossary

Actinic Light (page 65). A source of light especially rich in blue, violet, and ultraviolet rays. It has the property of hardening a light sensitive emulsion, chemically changing it from a soluble to an insoluble state.

Ammonium Bichromate (page 67). A salt used in the preparation of solutions which causes photographic emulsions to become sensitive to the actinic action of light. Also called ammonium dichromate.

Art (page 73). See **Copy.**

Autographic Print (page 9). A signed print produced entirely by the artist from original sketch to finished product. It's usually confined to limited editions.

Baseboard (page 10). A flat board or table top to which the screen frame is hinged; it's commonly referred to as a "bed."

Bed (page 126). See **Baseboard.**

Benday (page 65). A method (named after its inventor, Benjamin Day) whereby dots, textures, and other shading effects are introduced into art work by photographic means.

Binder (page 91). A gum, resin, or other substance in the vehicle of the ink. When dry this substance anchors the pigment particles to the printed surface.

Blacklight (page 97). A common name for ultraviolet rays within the wavelength range of 3,200 and 4,000 Angstrom units. Blacklight, in the form of fluorescent tubes, is used to expose carbon tissue and other photostencil film tissue. It's also used as a light source for prints made with fluorescent inks.

Blocking Out (page 29). The process in which an impervious film forming compound or other masking medium is applied to the screen fabric to prevent the penetration of ink. Same as **Masking Out.**

Blockout Compound (page 38). Glue, lacquer, shellac or another substance used in stencil preparation to close up parts of the open screen. Same as **Fill-in Compound.**

Blu-Film (page 60). A trade name for a handcut lacquer stencil film, usually blue in color.

Bolting Cloth. A resilient fabric woven with interlocking threads of natural silk; when stretched on a frame it becomes the screen for the stencil. Originally used by Swiss, Dutch and French millers for sifting and grading flour, silk bolting cloth has been widely adopted by the screen printing industry throughout the world, as one of the principal screen fabrics.

"Burning" the Film (page 126). A shop term which refers to inadvertently dissolving the edges of a film stencil image.

Carbon Arc Lamp (page 70). An intense and steady source of light produced when an electric current arcs or jumps across a pair of carbon rods which serve as electrodes. Because of their strong actinic effect on light sensitive material, carbon arc lamps rank among the favorite exposure light units used in the graphic arts.

Carbon Tissue (page 76). A specially-dyed emulsion or other pigmented material, coated onto a paper support, used in photostencil preparation. It's sometimes referred to as double transfer phototissue.

Colloid (page 29). Referring to photostencil technology, a colloid is a water-soluble, noncrystalline, film forming substance such as gelatin, glue, or albumin of very fine granules. It has the property of becoming light sensitive by the addition of a bichromate.

Color Separation (page 129). A photographic or manual method of separating distinct color areas in multicolor art. In photographic work, a "color separation" is a camera-produced negative in which a desired color has been recorded in black and white by using a special filter which is blind to all other colors in the art. In handmade color separations, the stencilmaker visually selects the distinct color areas in the art so that they can be prepared as separate, yet coordinated stencils.

Contact Screen (page 73). See **Halftone Screen.**

Continuous Tone (page 105). A range of unlimited tones from white to black without the use of dots or other mechanical patterns.

Copy (page 73). Refers to any matter to be reproduced. This includes typography, art work, photos, etc. In the terminology of screen printing, the word ''original art'' is often used as the equivalent of copy.

Crocking (page 121). The degree to which printed fabric will rub or wear off due to abrasion.

Crossmarks (page 79). See **Register Marks.**

Driers (page 92). Heavy metallic compounds of cobalt, lead, or manganese. When added to oxidizing inks, they act as catalysts to accelerate drying time.

Emulsion (page 67). A viscous solution consisting of finely divided particles more or less permanently suspended in a liquid, without actually being dissolved. The term is used in ink as well as in photostencil technology.

Extender Base (pages 101, 103). An inert substance used mainly to increase the volume of ink. Extender base is also used to make the ink mixture heavier and more transparent. It's similar to transparent base, but lacks its purity and vaseline-like property.

Feed (pages 110, 111). The act of placing the stock to be printed in the register guides on the printing bed.

Fill-in Compound (page 38). See **Blockout Compound.**

Flock (pages 9, 17, 98). Short, hair-like fibers of wool, cotton, nylon, silk, or other material. These are dusted or otherwise applied to a tacky surface. Flock is used to produce the effect of suede, plush, velour, fur, etc.

Flood Stroke (page 111). A double stroke of the squeegee; the first stroke scoops up the ink and lightly skims over the surface of the screen while it's in a raised position; the return stroke, with the screen lowered, bears down with full pressure and produces the actual impression. The flood stroke principle is used in most automatic screen printing presses and yields sharper printing results.

Four Color Process (page 89). A sequence of printings from a series of four halftone photostencils, one for each color (yellow, red, blue, and black). By this process any multicolor art can be reduced to just four printings, yet retain all—or nearly all—colors in the original art.

Gang Up (page 142). Identical design units repeated and positioned on one large sheet to economize on printing time. After printing, the individual units are cut and separated. Ganging up is also adaptable to design units which are dissimilar, provided the colors are the same.

Gelatin (page 65). A substance derived from animal tissue, bones, hoofs, or vegetable proteins, used in the preparation of photographic compounds as well as film stencil sheets.

Guides (pages 35, 42). Small tabs of cardboard, metal, or other material fastened to the bed against which the stock to be printed is registered in a predetermined position. Alternate terms: register guides, grippers, and stoppers.

Halftone (pages 66, 73). In relation to photostencils, a halftone is a positive or negative produced in dot textures representing graduated tones and blends.

Halftone Screen (page 73). A glass plate or other transparent surface upon which uniform opaque lines are etched in fine grid formation. The apertures between the lines photographically convert continuous tones into graduated dot patterns.

Hand (page 122). A term used in textile printing, referring to the degree of softness or flexibility of the fabric after printing.

Hickey. A speck of dirt, lint, or other obstruction in the printing area which shows up as a negative spot on the print.

Inert Pigment (page 91). A powdery substance (usually lacking in opacity) which is added to pure color pigments to extend the volume of ink. In addition it endows the ink with certain desirable working properties.

Law of Inverse Squares (page 75). Used when referring to photographic exposures. The amount of light of a point source falling on an object is inversely proportional to the square of the distance from the source to the object.

Law of Simultaneous Contrast (page 101). Colors are influenced in hue by adjacent colors. Each color imparts to its neighbor a tinge or cast of its own complement, that is, its opposite on the color wheel.

Line Copy (page 66). Pictorial composition, lettering, or type delineated as lines, solids, or dotted textures. These can be reproduced by photographic or hand-prepared screens, depending on the detail involved.

Line Negative (or **Line Positive,** page 66). Transparencies for photostencils made from line copy.

Long Ink. An ink that flows freely; it's usually slow drying.

Maskoid (page 44). A trade name for a fluid rubber cement type of substance used in resist stencils.

Unlike tusche, maskoid is peeled or rubbed off, rather than dissolved.

Metal-Clad Laminate (page 146). In electronic circuitry, this term is used to designate a sheet of copper or other conductive metal laminated to an insulating board made of phenolic plastic or other nonconductive material.

Mineral Spirits (page 100). A petroleum distillate such as benzine, Varsol, or Varnolene, used as a solvent and thinner for oil based paints.

Moiré. An astigmatic pattern resulting from the superimposition of two or more halftone screens on mesh fabrics.

Monofilament (page 22). A screen fabric in which each thread of the mesh is made up of a single fiber or filament. Nylon and stainless steel are examples of monofilament screen fabrics.

Multifilament (page 121). A screen fabric in which each thread of the mesh is made up of several separate fibers or filaments twisted to form the structure of the thread. Natural silk and dacron are examples of multifilament screen fabrics.

Negative (page 41). A photographic image which reverses the black and white relationship of the original copy, as distinguished from a positive where the relationship is retained.

Nu-Film (page 60). A trade name for a handcut lacquer film tissue.

Off-Contact Printing (page 113). A makeready in the screen setup enabling the screen fabric to lift off the printed surface just as soon as the squeegee passes over it. Off-contact printing produces sharper impressions because it eliminates screen drag.

One-Hand Squeegee (page 25). A squeegee constructed with a grip handle in the center. In use, the squeegee handle is gripped with the right hand in the right to left movement across the screen; with the left hand in the left to right movement across the screen.

Opaquing (page 71). Blocking out portions of photographic positives (or negatives) with an opaquing compound to make them impervious to light.

Original (page 73). See **Copy.**

Overdraw (page 78). In the preparation of stencils for multicolor work, a very small marginal extension of one color onto another is made to assure perfect register control.

Oxidation (page 92). Used with reference to a principle of drying generally associated with oil based inks. Oxidation is the process of drying in which the oil in the ink chemically combines with oxygen in the air to form a hard, insoluble ink film.

Pack-Up (page 75). A built-up surface consisting of a thick piece of cardboard or other material smaller in size than the inside dimensions of the printing screen. It's used to provide better contact between screen fabric and film tissue or photopositive in stencil preparation.

Photoflood Light Bulbs (pages 67, 70). A simple light source for exposing photostencils, photoflood bulbs are of high intensity, fit into ordinary light sockets, and have a lightlife of two to six hours.

Pigment (page 91). A basic ingredient in the ink mixture, composed of fine particles of coloring matter derived from plant, animal or vegetable sources, or by a synthetic process.

Plasticizer (pages 93, 97). A substance added to tempera paint, dye compounds, or other mixtures to make them more flexible and often to improve their working properties.

Polymerization (page 92). Referring to a principle of drying, polymerization is the process in which drying takes place when two or more molecular units of a resin link up to form larger units or chains. This results in the formation of a strong and flexible ink film.

Positive (pages 41, 65, 66). A photographic image which retains the black and white relationship of the original copy, as distinguished from a negative which reverses the relationship.

Printed Circuit (pages 97, 99, 145). An electronic panel in which the wiring elements are composed of a schematic pattern of electrically conductive strips produced by means of a printing process.

Process Camera (page 73). A precision built, fine-focus camera used to produce negatives and positives, both in line and halftone.

Profilm (pages 10, 60). A trade name for a handcut film which, in its original development, required heat to be adhered to the screen fabric. Today, nearly all handcut stencil films (including Profilm) are adhered to the screen with an adhering fluid.

Progressive Proofs (page 87). In multicolor printing, the term refers to a series of color proofs showing an impression of each color printed in the proper sequence. Colloquially called "progs."

Pushpin Hinge (page 19). Sometimes referred to as a slip-pin hinge. A two part hinge held in an interlocking position by a fitted pin or rod, it's used to attach the screen frame to the printing bed. When the pin is removed, the two parts separate to allow the screen to be disengaged from the bed.

Reclaiming the Screen (page 37). Washing out or otherwise removing the design image on the screen to clear the fabric for a new stencil.

Reducer (page 100). A varnish, oil, or solvent, which, when added to an ink mixture, reduces its viscosity. If used in moderation, it doesn't materially alter the chromatic value of the color.

Register (page 128). The exact positioning of the design image on the printing surface, a matter of special importance in multicolor work.

Register Marks (page 77). Fine crosslines drawn on the art and duplicated on each stencil to facilitate fitting one color over another in perfect alignment.

Resin (page 92). An amorphous solid or semi-solid organic substance of natural or synthetic origin, dissolved in a compatible vehicle. It serves as a binding agent for the pigment.

Retarder (page 96). An additive for printing ink used to slow down drying properties.

Rubylith (page 71). A trade name for a ruby-colored film tissue laminated to a transparent backing sheet, used in preparing handcut photopositives and negatives.

Run (page 107). A shop term referring to the actual printing procedure or the extent of an edition, as in the expressions, "the beginning of a run", "run the job", or "a long run."

Safelight (page 65). A red, yellow, or amber light bulb of small wattage which provides convenient work illumination, yet has a negligible actinic effect on light-sensitive material.

Screen (page 126). In the context of screen printing, the term *screen* refers to silk or other fabric stretched on a printing frame. The term is often used synonymously with *stencil,* as in the expression "wash the screen." In the context of the graphics arts in general, the term *screen* refers to a photographic or mechanical dot pattern, as in the expressions "65-line screen", "halftone screen", or "benday screen." "halftone screen", or "benday screen."

Sensitizer (page 65). Generally refers to a bichromate solution which when added to a photographic colloid, such as gelatin, renders it sensitive to the actinic action of light.

Serigraphy (page 13). A term occasionally used for screen printing as a creative art medium to differentiate it from its application as a commercial reproduction process.

Shading Sheets (page 89). Transparent sheets with imprinted lines, dots, or other patterns, used for obtaining tonal effects in photographic reproduction processes.

Short Ink (page 103). A nonspreading ink—one that "stays put" when printed. This is usually a desirable working property in screen ink formulations since it produces sharp printing results.

Sizing (pages 37, 38). A thin solution of glue or starch, applied to the screen fabric to temporarily close the mesh.

Slip-pin Hinge (page 19). See **Push-pin Hinge.**

Split Fountain (page 89). A technique in which two or more non-adjacent colors are printed simultaneously. This is made possible by partitioning the screen into compartments. Each compartment is printed with a separate color and separate squeegee.

Squeegee (pages 10, 17, 25). A rubber-bladed implement used in forcing the ink through the openings of a stencil. The term refers to the total implement or to the rubber blade in particular, as in the expression "sharpen the squeegee."

Stock (page 35). A broad connotation referring to paper, cardboard, glass, metal or whatever material is to be printed.

Strike Sheet (page 124). A prerun proof or sample submitted for approval before proceeding with the actual run; a term used mostly in fabric printing.

Take-off (page 107). The act of removing the wet print from the bed and placing it on a rack or other drying device. Usually this is the job of an assistant who in the trade is called a "take-off man."

Thinner (page 103). A shortened term for lacquer thinner. It generally encompasses wash thinner, adhering thinner, and various diluents and solvents for lacquer and other nitrocellulose compounds.

Toner (pages 100, 103). A highly concentrated pigment color mostly used in conjunction with transparent base to produce transparent tints.

Transparent Base (page 100, 103). The clear vaseline-like substance which when added to an ink mixture reduces its opacity, thickens its flow, and extends its volume.

Trapping. Printing one color over another in order to obtain compound colors or tones, by using transparent inks.

Tusche (pages 10, 44). A black, slightly greasy compound in liquid or crayon form used as one of the principal resist media in stencil preparation.

Two-Hand Squeegee (page 25). A squeegee constructed to be manipulated by gripping the casing with both hands at the same time.

Ulano Film (page 10). A trade name for various types of handcut and photographic films manufactured by Ulano Companies.

Underside of the Screen (page 75). The lower side of the screen, the one which comes in contact with the stock being printed.

Vacuum Bed (page 109). A printing bed, the surface of which has hundreds of tiny holes through which air is sucked by means of a vacuum pump. During the printing interval, the paper or other stock is held to the bed by the action of the vacuum pump, resulting in better register and sharper printing.

Vacuum Contact Frame (page 70). A unit used in photoscreen exposures whereby perfect contact between a light-sensitive material and a positive is established by the suction action of a pump device.

Varnish (pages 38, 39). Usually refers to oil which has been modified by heat and the addition of certain gums, resins, or other material to reduce the viscosity of the ink mixture and/or to cause it to dry with a gloss finish.

Varnolene (page 100). A trade name for a volatile solvent, produced by distilling crude petroleum oils. Varnolene evaporates faster than kerosene, but not nearly as fast as naptha, benzine or turpentine.

Vehicle (page 91). The liquid part of an ink mixture containing a binder of oil, resin, or gum and a compatible solvent.

American and British Suppliers

Many art and sign supply stores carry a limited assortment of screen printing material—screen frames, squeegees, screen fabrics, inks, solvents, and so on. A more extensive selection is available through national manufacturers and dealers, some of whom are listed below.

The following is by no means meant to be a comprehensive directory, nor should it be assumed that it reflects the personal preference of the author. The compilation of names is based primarily on the frequency with which the firms' products and services appear in the advertising pages and news columns of *Screen Printing Magazine,* the chief trade journal of the industry in the United States.

Quite a number of suppliers who carry a general line of screen supplies and equipment publish illustrated catalogs intended for professional personnel in industry and schools.

General Line of Supplies and Equipment

Active Process Supply Company, Inc.
15 W. 20th St., New York, N.Y. 10011

Advance Process Supply Company
400 N. Noble St., Chicago, Ill. 60622

Atlas Silk Screen Supply Company
1733 Milwaukee Ave., Chicago, Ill. 60647

Becker Sign Supply Company
319 N. Paca St., Baltimore, Md.

California Process Supply Company
2836 Tenth St., Berkeley, Calif.

Colonial Printing Ink Company
180 E. Union Ave., E. Rutherford, N.J. 07073

The Jay Products Company
2868 Colerain Ave., Cincinnati, Ohio 45225

Charles M. Jessup Company
22 N. 26th St., Kenilworth, N.J.

KC-Atlanta Color Corporation
1264 Logan Circle, N.W., Atlanta, Ga. 30318

Martin Supply Company
619-25 W. Franklin St., Baltimore, Md.

The Naz-Dar Company, Inc.
1087 N. Branch St., Chicago, Ill. 60622

Pan-American Supply Company
2525 N.W. 75th St., Miami, Fla. 33147

Jos. E. Podgor Company, Inc.
P.O. Box 1714, Philadelphia, Pa. 19105

Process Supply Company
762 Hanley Ind. Court, St. Louis, Mo. 63144

Rayco Paint Company
2535 N. Laramie Ave., Chicago, Ill. 60639

Regional Sign Supply Company
352 Paxton Ave., Salt Lake City, Utah 84101

Screen Process Supplies Mfg. Company
1199 E. 12th St., Oakland, Calif.

Seracreen Corporation
5-25 47th Rd., Long Island City, N.Y. 11101

Texas Screen Process Supply
325 N. Walton St., Dallas, Texas

Manufacturers and Dealers of Presses and Related Equipment

American Screen Process Equipment Company
404 N. Noble St., Chicago, Ill. 60622

Cincinnati Printing & Drying Systems, Inc.
1111 Meta Dr., Cincinnati, Ohio 45237

Denco Manufacturing, Inc.
8727 Narragansett Ave., Morton Grove, Ill. 60053

Ernst W. Dorn Company, Inc.
145 W. 22nd St., Los Angeles, Calif. 90007

General Research, Inc.
309 S. Union Ave., Sparta, Mich. 49345

Graphic Equipment of Boston
22 Simmons St., Boston, Mass. 02120

Lawson Printing Machinery Company
4434 Olive Blvd., St. Louis, Mo. 63108

M & M Research Engineering Company
13111 W. Silver Spring Drive, Butler, Wis. 53007

Pace Manufacturing Company
2002 34th St., Des Moines, Iowa

Pan Industrial Corp.
212 Fifth Ave., New York, N.Y. 10016

Photo Process Screen Mfg. Company
179-189 W. Berks St., Philadelphia, Pa. 19122

Pierce Specialized Equipment Company
1000 Varian St., San Carlos, Calif. 94070

Precision Screen Machinery Company
44 Utter Ave., Hawthorne, N.J. 07506

Manufacturers of Inks and Related Supplies

K. C. Coatings, Inc.
500 Railroad Ave., N. Kansas City, Mo. 64116

Colonial Printing Ink Company
180 E. Union Ave., E. Rutherford, N.J. 07073

Cudner & O'Connor Company
4035 W. Kinzie St., Chicago, Ill. 60624

Excello Color & Chemical Company
400 N. Noble St., Chicago, Ill. 60622

General Formulations
320 S. Union Ave., Sparta, Mich. 49345

Iddings Paint Company, Inc. (tempera paints)
45-30 38th Ave., Long Island City, N.Y. 11101

The Naz-Dar Company
1087 N. Branch St., Chicago, Ill. 60622

Radiant Color Company
2800 Radiant Ave., Richmond, Calif. 94804

Sherwin-Williams Company
101 Prospect Ave., N.W., Cleveland, Ohio 44101

Sinclair & Valentine
1212 Avenue of the Americas, New York, N.Y. 10036

Switzer Brothers, Inc., Day-Glo Color Division
4732 St. Clair Ave., Cleveland, Ohio 44103

Union Ink Company, Inc.
455 Broad Ave., Ridgefield, N.J. 07657

Wornow Process Paint Company
1218 Long Beach Ave., Los Angeles, Calif. 90021

Manufacturers of Handcut and Photostencil Films

Craftint Manufacturing Company
18510 Euclid Ave., Cleveland, Ohio 44112

E. I. duPont deNemours & Company, Inc.
2420-17 Nemours Building, Washington, Del.

McGraw Colorgraph Company
175 W. Verdugo Ave., Burbank, Calif. 91503

Nu-Film Products Company, Inc.
56 W. 22nd St., New York, N.Y. 10010

Ulano Products Company, Inc.
210 E. 86th St., New York, N.Y. 10028

Photographic Equipment

Miller-Trojan Company, Inc.
1083 W. Main St., Troy, Ohio

nuArc Company, Inc.
4100 W. Grand Ave., Chicago, Ill. 60651

Photo Emulsions and Related Supplies

Chroma Glo, Inc.
4832 Grand Ave., Duluth, Minn. 55807

Eastman Kodak Company
Rochester, N.Y. 14650

McGraw Colorgraph Company
175 W. Verdugo Ave., Burbank, Calif. 91503

Process Research, Inc.
2755 N. Rockwell St., Chicago, Ill. 60647

Roberts & Porter, Inc.
49-16 Newton Rd., Long Island City, N.Y. 11103

Wire Cloth Enterprises, Inc.
130 Gamma Dr., R.I.D.C. Industrial Park,
    Pittsburgh, Pa. 15238

Textile Supplies and Colors

Active Process Supply Company, Inc.
15 W. 20th St., New York, N.Y. 10011

American Crayon Company
167 Wayne St., Jersey City, N.J. 07303

CIBA Chemical & Dye Company
Fairlawn, N.J.

Inmont Corp., Color & Chemicals Division
150 Wagaraw Road, Hawthorne, N.J. 07506

Print Tables & Equipment Corp.
   (Screen Printing Tables)
340 Elmwood Terrace, Linden, N.J. 07036

Specialists in Screen Fabrics

Majestic Bolting Cloth Corp.
470 Park Avenue S., New York, N.Y. 10016

F. H. Paul & Stein Bros., Inc.
235 Fifth Ave., New York, N.Y. 10016

Tobler, Ernst & Traber, Inc.
420 Saw Mill River Road, Elmsford, N.Y. 10523

Wire Cloth Enterprises Inc.
130 Gamma Dr., R.I.D.C. Industrial Park,
    Pittsburgh, Pa. 15238

Phototypesetting Equipment and Services

Ace Clearprint Products, Inc.
42 E. 20th St., New York, N.Y. 10016

Filmotype Corp.
5700 McCormick Blvd., Stokie, Ill.

Martin J. Weber Studio
171 Madison Ave., New York, N.Y. 10016

Simmon Omega, Inc., Phototypesetting Division
P.O. Box 1060, Woodside, N.Y. 11377

StripPrinter, Inc.
Box 18-895 Oklahoma City, Okla. 73118

Varigraph Inc.
14410 Martin St., Madison, Wis.

The list of British firms below, is culled from a select directory of screen printing manufacturers and dealers given in *Practical Screen Printing* by Stephen Russ, reprinted here with the permission of the publishers, Watson-Guptill Publications, New York and Studio Vista, London.

General Supplies and Equipment

Ashworth-Lyme Marquetry
Old Corn Mill, Newton, New Mills,
  via Stockport, Cheshire

Dane & Company, Ltd.
1-2 Sugar House Lane, Stratford, London E15

George Hall (Sales) Ltd.
Beauchamp St., Shaw Heath, Stockport, Cheshire

T. N. Lawrence & Son Ltd.
2-4 Bleeding Heart Yard, Greville St.,
  Hatton Garden, London EC1

E. T. Marler Ltd.
191 Western Road, Merton Abbey, London SW19

D. O. Nicoll Ltd.
50 Britton St., London EC1

Pronk, Davis & Rusby Ltd.
44 Penton St., London N1

Screen Process Supplies Ltd.
24 Parsons Green Lane, London SW6

Selectasine Silk Screens Ltd.
22 Bulstrode St., London W1

Screen Inks

Blackwell and Co., Ltd.
Sugar House Lane, Stratford, London E15

A. G. W. Britton
Shenton St., Old Kent Road, London SE15

Cellon Ltd.
Kingston-on-Thames, Surrey

Coates Brothers, Ltd.
Easton St., Rosebery Ave., London WC1

John T. Keep & Sons Ltd.
15 Theobald's Road, London WC1

M. E. McCreary & Company
815 Lisburn Road, Belfast BT9 7GX

Skilbeck Brothers Ltd.
Bagnall House, 55 & 57 Glengall Road, London SE15

Winsor & Newton Ltd.
51 Rathbone Place, London W1

Photographic Supplies and Equipment

Kodak Ltd., Graphic Arts Sales Dept.
Kodak House, Kingsway, London WC2

Philips Electrical Ltd.
Century House, Shaftesbury Ave., London WC2

Textile Printing Equipment

E. G. K. (Textile Machinery & Accessories) Ltd.
256 Park Lane, Macclesfield, Cheshire

Macclesfield Engineering Co., Ltd.
Athey St., Macclesfield, Cheshire

Many of the American and a number of British firms have representative agencies in Canada, Mexico, France, Germany, Belgium, Switzerland, Italy, South Africa, Japan and other areas throughout the world. For addresses, write to the home offices of the parent firms listed or else communicate with the Screen Printing Association, International, 150 South Washington St., Falls Church, Va. 22046.

Annotated Bibliography

Listed below are reference works currently in print with a brief description of the contents of each one.

Auvil, Kenneth W., *Serigraphy: Silk Screen Techniques for the Artist,* Prentice-Hall Inc., Englewood Cliffs, N.J., 1965 (paperback).

An overview of the equipment and techniques of screen printing as a fine art.

Biegeleisen, J. I., *The Complete Book of Silk Screen Printing Production,* Dover Publications, New York 1963 (paperback).

A compendium on screen printing, with major emphasis on its industrial applications.

Biegeleisen, J. I. and Cohn, M. A., *Silk Screen Techniques,* Dover Publications, New York, 1958 (paperback).

A basic manual for printmakers on the screen process.

Carr, Francis, *A Guide to Screen Process Printing,* Studio Vista Books, London, 1961.

A survey of the process, by a lecturer associated with the London School of Printing. The book includes British Standards Specifications and a list of local suppliers.

Chieffo, Clifford T., *Silk Screen as a Fine Art,* Van Nostrand-Reinhold Publications Corp., New York, 1967.

A guide to the experimental and creative possibilities of screen printing as an art medium.

Fossett, R. O., *Techniques in Photography for the Screen Process Printer,* The Signs of the Times Publishing Co., Cincinnati, Ohio, 1959 (paperback).

A highly technical treatise on the principles and procedures of photographic stencil techniques.

Gilson, Thomas, *How to Print on Cylindrical and Contoured Surfaces,* The Jay Products Co., New York, 1962 (paperback).

A twenty-seven page monograph for the specialist in screen printing on containers and other three dimensional objects.

Kinsey, Anthony, *Introducing Screen Printing,* Watson-Guptill Publications, New York, 1968.

A ninety-six book devoted mainly to experimental textures and effects of special interest to art students and printmakers.

Kosloff, Albert, *Photographic Screen Process Printing,* The Signs of the Times Publishing Co., Cincinnati, Ohio, 1968.

A full treatment of material, procedures, and techniques for photographic screen printing.

Kosloff, Albert, *Screen Printing Electronic Circuits,* The Signs of the Times Publishing Co., Cincinnati, Ohio, 1968.

A technical treatise on the latest developments in screen printing of electronic circuitry.

Kosloff, Albert, *Textile Screen Printing,* The Signs of the Times Publishing Co., Cincinnati, Ohio, 1966.

Equipment and procedures used in the industrial screen printing of fabrics.

Russ, Stephen, *Fabric Printing by Hand,* Watson-Guptill Publications, New York, 1966.

A description of basic tools and materials for printing fabrics by hand or by press with a special chapter on screen printing techniques.

Russ, Stephen, *Practical Screen Printing,* Watson-Guptill Publications, New York, 1969.

A general survey of the process by a British craftsman and teacher.

Searle, Valerie and Clayson, Roberta, *Screen Printing on Fabric,* Watson-Guptill Publications, New York, 1969.

A description of textile screening, with suggestions for design motifs.

Shokler, Harry, *Artists Manual for Silk Screen Printmaking,* Tudor Publishing Co., New York, 1960.

The fine art aspects of the process presented by a leading practitioner.

Steffen, Bernard, *Silk Screen,* Pitman Publishing Company, New York, 1963 (paperback).

A thirty-one page brochure on the process by a well known serigraphic artist.

Screen Printing Magazine is the monthly journal which carries general trade news, feature stories on the latest technical developments in the field, as well as informative advertising by leading manufacturers and dealers. It's available at art and sign supply stores, or by subscription from The Signs of the Times Publishing Co., 407 Gilbert Avenue, Cincinnati, Ohio 45202.

Screen Printing Association, International, 150 South Washington Street, Falls Church, Va. 22046 is the industry's official trade organization, and serves as a clearing house for the dissemination of technical and business data.

Index

SILVER LAKE COLLEGE LIBRARY
Manitowoc, Wisconsin 54220

Edited by Diane C. Hines
Designed by James Craig and Robert Fillie
Graphic Production by Frank De Luca
Composed in nine point Helvetica Light by York Typesetting Company
Printed and bound by Halliday Lithographic Corporation